Published by Aperitifs Publishing Company
Santa Rosa, California
707-523-1611
johncburton@msn.com

ISBN: 978-1-7324530-0-5
Library of Congress number: 2018906908

Copyright: July 1, 2018
Written by;
John C. Burton
John Louder

Printed in the United States of America

All rights reserved. No part of this book may be reproduced or transformed in any form or by any means, electronic or mechanical, including photocopying, recording or by any information storage and/or retrieval system without permission in writing from the author or publisher.

Every attempt has been made to provide accurate information on the following subjects.

johncburton@msn.com
707-523-1611

FRONT COVER IMAGE
Cover image of Jackson's Napa Soda "Don't Get Roped In" with counterfeits 1906 calendar courtesy of Witherell Auctions, Sacramento Ca. (Brian Witherell) their great collector's book titled CALIFORNIA'S BEST with the Jackson image on page 225.

REAR COVER IMAGE
Both Richard Siri (Bartlett Springs reverse on glass) and Newell Snyder (Bartlett Springs letterhead) for allowing those items to be used in this reference book.

ACKNOWLEDGEMENTS
First and foremost, to Brian Witherell for allowing us to use the great *Jackson's Napa Soda "Don't Don't Get Roped In" with counterfeits* 1906 calendar. The calendar makes the book an instant success.

John Louder who co-authored this endeavor and supplied many bottles and historical information and spent many hours at the Sonoma County Library on 3rd street in Santa Rosa.

Richard Siri who allowed us to film his great *Bartlett Mineral Springs* reverse-on-glass sign, his Jackson Mineral Water match safe, his Astorg bottle, Haas Napa Soda bottle and a Jackson Napa Soda Bottle with the letters A & B on the bottom of the bottle.

Rick Siri who graciously allowed us to film his Lake County bottles; aqua Adam's Springs Mineral Water quart, Highland Mineral Water, amber Jackson's Napa Soda quart, aqua Samuel Soda Natural Mineral Water quarts, Witter Springs label and brochure.

Frank & Laurel Ritz for the photo of their rare Healdsburg Litton Healdsburg bottle.

Newall Snyder for the great Bartlett Springs advertisements, Bartlett Springs serving trays, and Napa Soda stock certificate.

Jeff Wichmann proprietor of American Bottle Auctions for use of photos from his past auction catalogs.

Especially to the on-line California Digital Newspaper where we found related items in the San Francisco Call, The Daily Alta and Sacramento Daily Union and the Santa Rosa Press Democrat.

And most importantly to Kathrine J. Rinehart, M. A.; Simone Kremkau, MLIS; Joanna Kolosov; MLIS at the Sonoma County Library History & Genealogy Center here in Santa Rosa who always graciously assists in our projects and directs us to additional information that helps make any project creditable.

John C. Burton
John Louder

TABLE OF CONTENTS

Stage in front of Santa Rosa House 1877	Page 1
James P. Clark's Stage Coach Line Handbill	Page 2
Stage coach images	Page 3
Stage leaving Adams Springs & Auto Stage heading to Geysers	Page 4
Ferry boat transportation	Page 5
Ferry boat carrying trains and docking in Marin County	Page 6
Image of Eureka ferry boat & crowd at Santa Rosa train station	Page 7
Adams Springs	Page 8
Adams Springs Mineral Water bottles	Page 9
Astorg Mineral Springs	Page 11
Aetna Springs	Page 13
Allen Springs	Page 17
Bartlett Springs	Page 19
Bonanza Springs Humboldt Artesian Water	Page 28
Boyes Hot Springs	Page 29
California Seltzer Springs	Page 31
Calistoga Hot Springs	Page 38
Columbia Soda Works	Page 43
Duncan's Springs	Page 44
El Toro Natural Mineral Water	Page 45
Fetters Hot Springs	Page 46
Geyser's Sonoma County	Page 47
Golden West	Page 51
Golden West Soda Works Frank Paillet and E. Herve & P. Somps	Page 52
Golden West Soda Works J. Somps & J. Meillete	Page 53
Golden West Soda Works P. Somps	Page 54
Haas Brothers	Page 55
Harbin Springs	Page 56
Highland Springs	Page 57
Hoberg's Resort	Page 63
Howard Springs	Page 64
Humboldt Joseph P. Monroe	Page 67
Kenwood Warm Springs	Page 69
Lytton (Litton) Springs	Page 70
Mark West Springs	Page 75
Napa Soda Phil Caduc	Page 76
Napa Soda Samuel Phillips	Page 78
Napa Soda Louis Leloy	Page 79
Napa Soda Dr. J. Henry Wood	Page 81
Napa Soda Works Ed Henry	Page 83
Napa Soda Springs Litigations	Page 84
Napa Soda Springs John P. Jackson	Page 87
Parker Hill Mineral Water	Page 100
Pine Mountain Mineral Water	Page 103
Pope Valley Peter (Pierre) Guillaumes	Page 104

Preston John Kolling	**Page 106**
Priest Soda Springs	**Page 109**
Samuel Mineral Springs	**Page 113**
Seigler Springs	**Page 122**
Shadow Springs	**Page 124**
Skaggs Springs	**Page 125**
Tamalpais Mineral Water	**Page 127**
Tolenas Springs	**Page 128**
Vichy Springs Young's	**Page 129**
Vichy Springs Napa	**Page 130**
Wall's Springs Mirabel Park	**Page 132**
Walters Springs	**Page 134**
White Sulphur Springs AKA Kawana Springs	**Page 135**
White Sulphur Springs (Blue Rock Springs) Vallejo	**Page 136**
Witter Springs	**Page 138**
Recommended Books	**Page 141**
Witherell & American Bottle auctions	**Page 142**
Organizations & Show Chair Persons	**Page 143**
1915 Listing of California Springs by Gerald A. Waring	**Page 144**

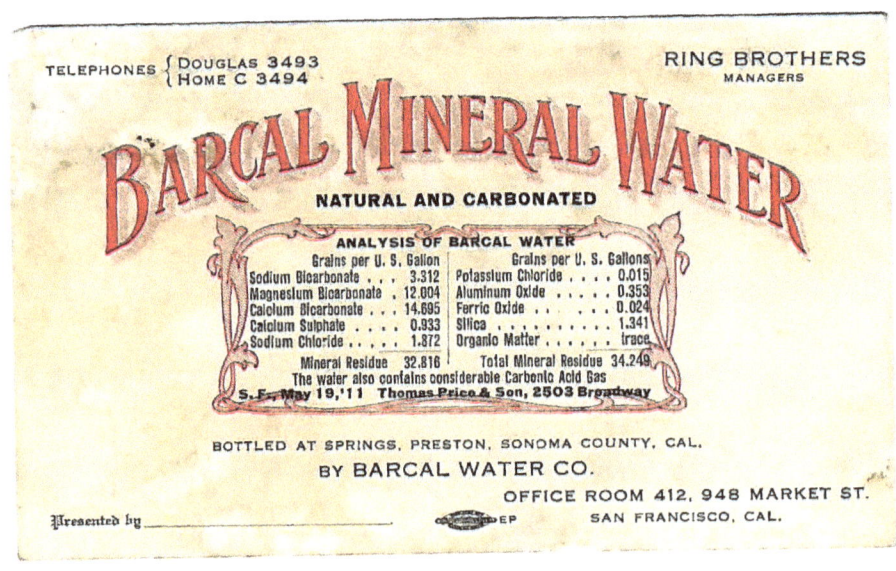

TRAVEL TO AND FROM THE SPRINGS

We get locked in traffic in the "Novato Narrows" and get frustrated. Let's look back at travel from San Francisco or Oakland to the springs in Lake County in the late 1880's.

In San Francisco we start at 7 a.m. leaving the Ferry Building on Market Street on a Ferry crossing to Sausalito. We transfer to a train in San Rafael then arrive in Cloverdale about noon. Now we board a stage coach and arrive at one of the springs about 4 p.m.

It's a complete day's outing travelling to Lake County from San Francisco or Oakland. The ferry's not bad if the bay is not choppy and you don't get seasick. If you do get seasick the motion on the train won't help you very much, however, the train ride is probably the most comfortable part of the adventure. Now bouncing and swaying in a stage coach that is jam-packed with passengers and luggage. No wonder you felt relaxed soaking in one of the springs the next day.

Stage in front of Santa Rosa House 1877
Sonoma County Library Collection

STAGE COACH HANDBILL SANTA ROSA TO CALISTOGA

Sonoma County Library Collection

**Onward to one of the springs.
Cheap seats on top of stage.
Sonoma County Library Collection**

**Stage leaving in front of Geyserville Hotel for Skaggs Springs Circa 1910
Sonoma County Library Collection**

Stage leaving Adam's springs 1915
Sonoma County Library Collection

Progress in the making circa 1909
Sonoma County Library Collection

TRANSPORTATION BY FERRY BOAT AND RAILROAD TO THE NORTHERN STAGE STOPS.

Ferry Building San Francisco 1886
Sonoma County Library Collection

Ferry boat Solano waiting for trains to on-load.
Trains backed on so they would be headed in the correct direction when leaving the Ferry.
Sonoma County Library Collection

Example of trains being transported across the bay by ferry
Sonoma County Library Collection

Land-dock connection for receiving trains in Marin
Sonoma County Library Collection

Ferries were named after northern California towns. Petaluma, Eureka, Contra Costa, Santa Rosa, Solano, Piedmont, Oakland, Emeryville, Vallejo, Etc.
Sonoma County Library Collection

Crowd at Santa Rosa Train Station at Railroad Square 1916
Sonoma County Library Collection

ADAMS SPRINGS

Adams Springs is located in Lake County approximately 8 miles southwest of Lower Lake. Adams springs was founded by Charles Adams who purchased the site in 1869. He immediately built a resort featuring his mineral water.

Dr. W. R. Prather purchased the property in 1908 built a hotel in 1927. The hotel could accommodate up to 400 persons. Also in 1908 a post office operated from 1908 until 1960. Dr. Prather is the person who bottled and sold mineral water.

Adams Springs Cottages and Hotel

ADAMS SPRINGS MINERAL WATER BOTTLES

FACE
(Both bottles)

ADAMS SPRINGS
MINERAL WATER
FOR STOMACH, LIVER AND KIDNEYS
LAKE COUNTY CALIFORNIA
DR. PRATHER PROP.

REVERSE

BLANK

Mineral Top **Crown Top**

Rick Siri collection **Burton collection**

SAN FRANCISCO CALL
June 23, 1903

Adams Springs

Why does Adams Springs, Lake County, get the crowd? Because it cures. It is the best water, has the best climate and gives the best service. Send for book of testimonials. Full particulars at Travelers' Information Bureau, 630 Market street, or by addressing
DR. W. R. PRATHER, Proprietor.

SAN FRANCISCO CALL
July 9, 1903

Fire Is Prevented From Communicating to Adjoining Buildings After a Hard Fight.

CALISTOGA, July 8.—The old hotel on the left side of the plaza at Adams Springs was totally destroyed by fire this afternoon, entailing a loss of about $5000. There are 250 guests at the springs, but fortunately no one was injured.

The fire spread rapidly through the hotel structure, but owing to an adequate supply of water and good pressure the flames were prevented from communicating to the adjoining buildings. The origin of the fire is not known.

ASTORG MINERAL WATER

Alphonse and Marcellin Astorg where butchers who owned a meat market at 108-5th Street in San Francisco. Antonio Astorg was a peddler who I imagine sold both meat and the mineral water. The family owned Astorg Mineral Water at Astorg Springs in Cobb Valley in Lake Country.

CROCKER-LANGLEY SAN FRANCISCO DIRECTORY

Astorg Alphonse, meat market, 108, 5th, and proprietor Astorg Springs, Cobb Valley, Lake Co., Cal., r. 108, 5th
" Antonie, peddler, r. 23 Aileen Av
" Marcellin, butcher Alphonse Astorg, r. 108, 5th

SAN FRANCISCO CALL
March 22, 1896

WANTED—FROM THE INTERIOR TOWNS, a good enterprising business commercial house for the agency for the finest mild delicious beverage, natural medicinal mineral water, on the earth from the Astorg Springs, Lake County, Cal.; the search of Ponce de Leon for the fountain of perpetual youth. Address A. ASTORG, 108 Fifth st.

WANTED—10-MULE TEAM TO HAUL THE mineral water from Astorg Springs. Apply A. ASTORG, 108 Fifth st.

SAN FRANCISCO CALL
May 24, 1894

ASTORG SPRING MINERAL WATER.

THE FOUNTAIN OF PERPETUAL YOUTH: cures most any disease of long standing; cured hundreds; recommended by thousands in four months in this city: no agents. A. ASTORG, 108 Fifth st., sole proprietor; Glenbrook Hotel, Lake County, one-quarter mile from spring, has privilege of the water.

SAN FRANCISCO CALL
September 30, 1910

ASTORG—In this city, September 30, 1910, Morcelin, beloved brother of Hyppolite and Alphonse Astorg, and uncle of Mr. and Mrs. T. Delbex and Mr. and Mrs. F. Alligino, and cousin of Mr. and Mrs. Camile Mailhebuan, a native of France, aged 59 years and 6 months.

Friends and acquaintances are respectfully invited to attend the funeral services Monday, October 3, 1910, at 9 o'clock a. m., at his late residence, 1605 Laguna street, thence to French church, where a mass will be said for the repose of his soul. Interment Holy Cross cemetery.

SAN FRANCISCO CALL
May 28, 1911

AGED BUTCHER'S DEAD BODY FOUND BY BOY

Alphonse Astorg Believed to Have Taken Strychnine

[Special Dispatch to The Call]

MARTINEZ, Oct. 4.—The body of Alphonse Astorg, an aged butcher, who has for the last year been living near Lafayette, was found on the Moraga grant last evening by Albert Carpenter, a boy, who was hunting in the hills. He called Lloyd Brown this morning, and the two visited the place, to find that the man, who was thought by young Carpenter to be intoxicated, had been dead for some time. It is believed that he came to his death by taking strychnine. He leaves a widow in Lafayette and was about 65 years of age, having resided in Walnut Creek and Lafayette for many years.

FACE		REVERSE
ASTORG MINERAL WATER		BLANK

Richard Siri collection

AETNA SPRINGS

Aetna Springs situated 16 miles from St. Helena was discovered in 1880's by John Lawley owner of the Aetna mine in Napa County. The resort and spa was developed by Len Owens and became a popular destination for vacationers and health seekers from the San Francisco Bay area. It also featured one of the first golf courses in 1891 west of the Mississippi. The resort closed June 2009 and was being renovated in 2012.

According to the San Francisco Directory Aetna had an array of distributors changing approximately every year or two.

- 1886 – 1887 A. F. Learned Agent located at 757½ Howard Street San Francisco
- 1887 – 1888 A. F. Cooper Agent located at 757½ Howard Street San Francisco
- 1888 – 1889 Len Owens & Bartlett 513 Montgomery Street San Francisco
- 1889 – 1899 Len Owens 106-108 Drumm Street San Francisco
- 1899 – 1900 Louis Klee & Linn 619 Montgomery Street San Francisco
- 1900 – 1901 Louis Klee & Company 604-608 Bryant Street San Francisco
- 1901 – 1903 Baumgarten & Company 604-608 Bryant Street San Francisco
- 1903 – 1904 Aetna Mineral Water Agency 7 Tenth Street San Francisco
- 1904 – 1905 Hilbert Mercantile 312 Market Street San Francisco
- 1905 -   Aetna Mineral Water Agency 140 Second Street San Francisco

AETNA SPRINGS POSTCARDS

Aetna Springs Main Facility

Aetna Springs Arbor

Aetna Springs Grounds

FACE	REVERSE

AETNA MINERAL WATER	AETNA MINERAL WATER |</br></br>

	BOTTOM	

AETNA MINERAL WATER TRADE MARK REGISTERED		AETNA MINERAL WATER TRADE MARK REGISTERED

FACE	REVERSE

AETNA **SODA WATER**	**NATURAL** **MINERAL WATER**

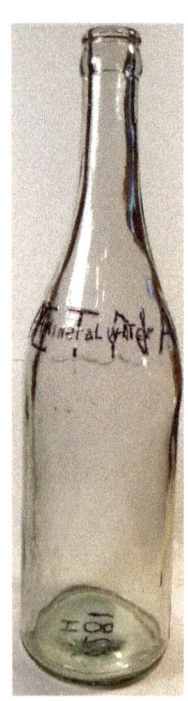

AETNA
MINERAL WATER

ALLEN SPRINGS

Allen Springs is located miles from Bartlett Springs operated by George and Vale Allen. On property is a two-story hotel, full restaurant and dining area, billiard saloon, barber shop, 21 cottages, and stables.

The springs consisted of iron springs, white Sulphur springs, and both cold fresh water springs. Their main clientele was not just tourism but also directed towards invalids. Allen Springs could be reached from either Sacramento or San Francisco by train to Williams then transferring to a stage coach for a 40-mile journey.

They bottled mineral water from their iron and Sulphur springs.

ALLEN SPRINGS

FACE
(Vertical)

```
M   A   W
I   L   A
N   L   T
E   E   E
R   N   R
A
L
```

REVERSE
Blank

BARTLETT SPRINGS

Bartlett Springs is located in Lake County approximately 10 miles north of Clearlake Oaks. Founded in 1869 by Green Bartlett he built a resort claiming that his spring water would cure all. His resort could accommodate approximately 500 guests at one time. The "in-house" post office operated from 1873 until 1935.

Reverse-on-glass Richard Siri collection

Postcard image of Bartlett Springs

BARTLETT WATER LABELS

        7 oz.   Quart

John Louder Painted Label Bottles

Bartlett water bottle case Richard Siri collection

BARTLETT SPRINGS BOTTLE

FACE

BARTLETT
SPRING
MINERAL WATER
CALIFORNIA

REVERSE

Blank

BARTLETT SPRINGS BOTTLING PLANT

A NOTE HOME

Bartlett Springs – Aug 25/21
Dear Etta, The scenery was grand all the way here. Lots of people here yet. Waters taste funny some tastes like gasoline at Adam's spring. Will be home soon. Mother is tired. Annie.

John Louder Postcard

BARTLETT SPRINGS WORK ORDER

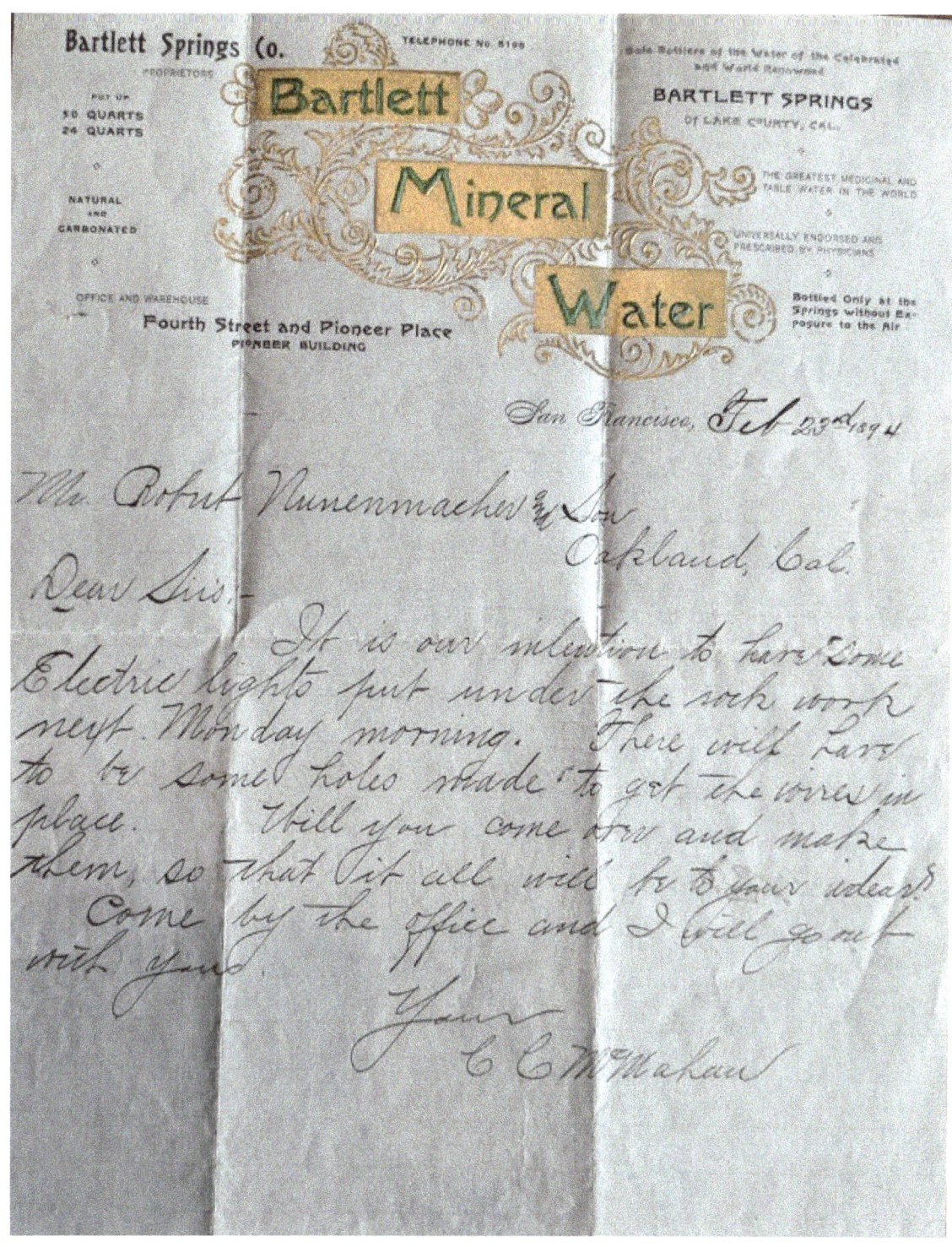

Newall Snyder collection

BARTLETT SPRINGS LETTERHEADS

Letterheads Newall Snyder collection

BARTLETT SPRINGS SERVING TRAYS

Trays Newall Snyder collection

BARTLETT SPRINGS ADVERTISEMENT

Newall Snyder collection

BARTLETT SPRINGS POSTCARDS

BONANZA SPRINGS

Located in the Cobb Mountain area of Lake County. In 1870 it is believed that the population was approximately 20 persons. The 1880 census brings it up to approximately 80 persons. Bonanza Springs is approximately two miles from Seigler Springs.

George M. Henderson bottled mineral water at the Bonanza Spring from 1880 to 1882.

FACE

G. M. HENDERSON'S
BONANZA
MINERAL WATER
MENDOCINO
CAL.

REVERSE

BLANK

BOYES HOT SPRINGS

As with all hot springs in northern California hot springs were used by the Native Americans as a recreation area and for medicinal purposes. In 1840 the springs were developed for commercial use for Anglo's by T. M. Leavenworth a resident of San Francisco. The springs were sold in 1889 to Captain H. E. Boyes who called the area Agua Rica and proceeded to build a hotel.

With the property having been sold to Theodor Richards and with John Kelly opened a bottling works February 10, 1906 manufacturing and selling Boyes Mineral Water.

In June 1908 John Kelly announced that John W. Goetz and Edward H. Spiro who were proprietors of Eureka California Soda Works in San Francisco and Isaac Spiro proprietor of Popular Soda Works in San Francisco of which both plants were destroyed in the 1906 earthquake were named agents for Boyes Mineral Water and they formed the Majestic Bottling Company in 1907 at 20 Biedman Street near Ellis in San Francisco.

It is estimated that approximately 1910 they expanded the Majestic label to flavors; orange grape, lemon, strawberry as well as ginger ale and soda water in crown top bottles

In May 1920 Kelly sold Boyes Water rights to a lady, Mrs. Peterson; however, Kelly retained rights to the bottling plant and added Orange Crush to his line of products.

Today the property is home of Sonoma Mission Inn and Spa a division of Fairmont Resorts and Hotels.

BOYES HOT SPRINGS MINERAL WATER

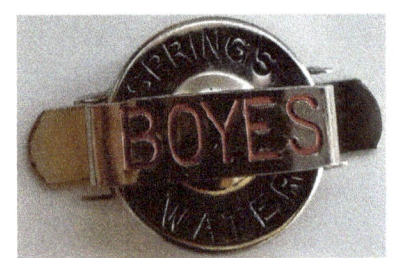

CALIFORNIA SELTZER SPRINGS
Cloverdale

Martin Heller & William T. Garratt
1875 - 1880

FACE

CALIFORNIA
NATURAL
SELTZER WATER

REVERSE

(BEAR)
H & G
(Heller & Garratt)

Richard Siri Collection

Daily Alta
June 26, 1870

CALIFORNIA SELTZER WATER is f st winning its way into popular favor. It can be obtained at Drug Stores, Saloons and Grocery Stores. or at the General Depot, KITZ & HILDEBRANDT, No. 223 Sacramento street. It is highly recommended by leading Physicians, and as a Cure for Dyspepsia, Indigestion, Diseases of the Liver and Kidneys, and for Indisposition peculiar to Females it has no equal. Try it, and it will recommend itself. For further information, see small bills. je23-tf

CALIFORNIA SELTZER SPRINGS

Daily Alta
October 9, 1870
Mendocino County, Oct. 3rd, 1870

Cloverdale: A small town situated at the upper end of Russian River Valley, eighteen miles from Healdsburg. This is the point where the two railroads will meet. There is considerable rivalry at present existing between the two companies, in trying to turn the tide of travel over their route. That the Petaluma party will succeed there is no doubt, as they have nearly completed their road to Santa Rosa, and another season will see it finished to this place, when the public will take more comfortable way of writing by rail than that of the old slow coach mode of traveling. On looking around a stranger wonders how he is to get out of the valley, is nothing but high and almost an accessible mountains met his gaze.

Meeting an "intelligent contraband," I inquired if there was any chance for me to get out of the valley, his answer was; "*Do-no massa: I come's here but couldn't buy my way out, so here I am massa: don't like de looks ob dem hills, may be all right: do-no.*"

Coming to the conclusion that I had sought information from the wrong man, I tried another." *Can you tell me how to get over those mountains?*" Said I. "*Yes I can: you go with me!*"
I went along with could not see how I was to get through those mountains. His seem to be by nature, the natural turnings of the railroad. Still, there is no doubt but that the echoing sounds of the iron horse as he screams along the mountain gorges on his way to the ocean, will ere long be heard, where now the wild deer and panther roam at will.

Following my guide, we soon arrived at the office of the Stage Company, where I was booked for an outside seat for this place. I have traveled over rough roads, during a residence for nearly 19 years on this coast but must accord to Mendocino County my fullest recognition as the banner County for bad roads. If the supervisors look to their own interests, they will remedy the evil at an early day.

After a ride of twelve miles over this break-neck Road, I arrived at the Fountain House, where I took passage on foot for the springs, one mile distant.

The California Seltzer Springs

Is about one mile from the fountain house which is situated on the Russian River. I speak only of it from my own experience. As a cure for indigestion, liver complaint, afflictions of the kidneys, etc., it has no equal. There are those who may accuse me of being prejudiced in favor of this water, but such is not the case. Of its curative properties I speak, as I said before, from experience. It cured me of a disease that the baffled the skill of the best physicians in San Francisco. This spring is as yet unknown to the world. Its many virtues are yet unheralded

On my arrival at The Springs I received a most cordial welcome from Mr. H. S. Byam and lady. Mr. Byam is the present proprietor of the spring, and the original discoverer of its medicinal qualities as curative water

The Springs

Four years since while riding through the valley looking for a stock ranch, he alighted from his horse to obtain a drink at the spring, the properties of which he immediately recognized upon drinking from its heretofore hidden depths

The Scenery

At the Springs is beyond my powers of description. Surrounded by hills on all sides, it speaks but a single word for nature, and that word is, "Beautiful!" The springs are situated about three hundred and fifty yards back of Mr. Byam's house, at the head of a small ravine. He has taken particular care to enclose the springs in such a manner as to preclude all possibility of the escape of gas. The size of the spring is four feet in diameter and three feet in depth, and discharges sixty gallons per hour. The analysis of the waters is as follows: free carbonic acid in abundance; bicarbonate of lime in abundance; bicarbonate of magnesia in abundance; bicarbonate of iron sparingly; chloride of sodium sparingly; chloride of magnesia in abundance and bicarbonate of soda in abundance.

The above is the State's Assayer's analysis of the water. Its medicinal qualities no one will doubt after reading the analysis. California abounds in mineral waters, but none have, as yet, been discovered that possess the combination of minerals equal to the California Seltzer Water. No place yet has been discovered that has the natural advantages of this spring. Situated, as it is, at the head of a ravine, whose beautiful waters flow through the peaceful valley below, with its groves of Laurel, is hills of natural Evergreen, and the sweet scented flowers, the California Seltzer Springs are sure to become a popular place of resort

It has eternal advantages which other springs do not possess. Aside from his curative qualities, the patient seeking is virtues can take his gun, and within five hundred yards of the spring can kill any amount of game, from a grizzly bear down to a coil. The soil is well adapted to raising grapes, and will become at no distant day, a great wine producing region. The California Seltzer Water was introduced into San Francisco, on the seventh day of last May, by J. R. Mains.

I do not propose to speak of its qualities here. It will speak for itself. Capitalists who are investing their money in mining stocks which to them are worth less than nothing, allows such chances for making a fortune to pass by, when the investment of a few hundred dollars would bring a return of thousands.

Since its introduction in San Francisco the demand has been greater than the present means of transportation. Still, when the railroad is finished Cloverdale, there will be but 12 miles travel from the spring. J. M. R.

Daily Alta
June 14, 1890

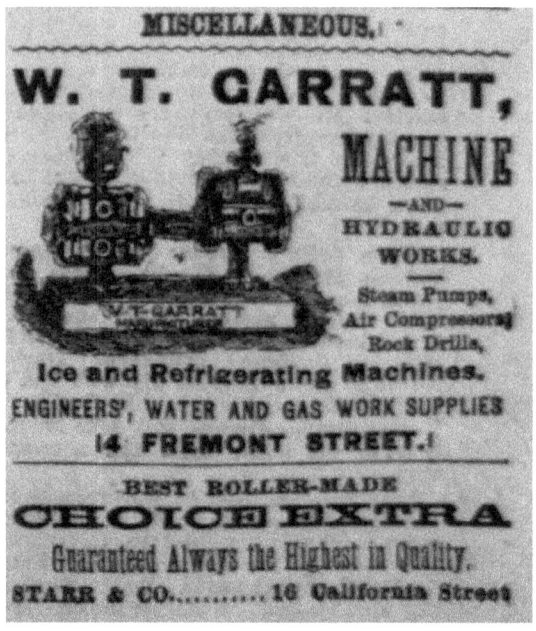

The will of the late William T. Garrett was filed for probate yesterday by the widow, and she Garrett, who, by the terms of the will, is appointed executor without bonds. The estate consist of real and personal property in this city and elsewhere, the value of which is unknown. Will was executed by the deceased on April 4, 1883, and was witnessed by George W. Gates and Archibald L. Taylor. Deceased bequeaths to his daughter, Mrs. Emma Vaughan, the residence property she now occupies; also, the springs and lands known as the California Seltzer Springs and the sum of $10,000.

To his daughter, Amelia C. Allen, the residence property she now occupies; also, a five-acre lot in Oakland and $10,000.

To Clara P. Morton, another daughter he bequeaths a lot on Howard Street, between Twenty-Second and Twenty-Third.

Julia W. Garratt, and unmarried daughter, gets a lot on Fremont Street, between Howard and Folsom, and $10,000 in money.

To Mary Alice Garratt, also a daughter, he leaves all the interest he possessed in two 50-vara lots on Bryant Street, between Fourth and Fifth.

The lands known as the tidelands are to be equally divided between Emma, Amelia, Clara, Julia and Mary Alice, hoping that it will be kept as a whole for many years to come.

To his brother, Benjamin F. Garratt, and sons, William and Milton, deceased bequeaths the business and real property corner of Fremont and Natoma streets, including buildings, land, tools and stock, together with stock in hands of agents; the monies bequeathed in a former will to be paid out testator on book accounts in three equal installments, one third in three years, his debts to be paid first, the balance to be equally divided or left as a whole to the firm of W. T. Garratt & Co., consisting of his brother Benjamin and sons William and Milton. The firm is to pay the father, Jose W. Garratt, $75 per month for life, pay $5,000 to his sister Rose and $3,000 to this Allen little, payable in three installments.

To his wife Anna he leaves all of his stock, consisting of insurance, railroad and steamboat and his life insurance, together with the Homestead property of every kind. His two sons are to have the land and building at 513 and 515 Market Street, near First, the wife to take charge and collect the rents, and to use the same if needed for the benefit of sons. All property, real and personal, not mentioned, goes to the widow.

In case the widow dies the property, real and personal, is to be divided as: the daughter, Emma, gets the life insurance in the Connecticut mutual, which amounts to $10,000. Amelia is to have the stock in the California Steam Navigation Company, except 100 shares, which go to Domingo Marcucci. Claire is to have one-half interest in the lots and building now used as a homestead at 405 Sixth Street, the other have to be divided between the two sons-in-law, William A. Allen and James Bond. They are also to have the books in the library and the bookcase. The portraits of the family go to each as painted for them. The one painted by Nahl goes to his son William, and the one by Wise to Milton the brother gets the scrapbooks

** Note that this may be the seed for Garrett Hardware in Healdsburg and Windsor.

CALIFORNIA NATURAL SELTZER WATER

FACE

CALIFORNIA
NATURAL
SELTZER WATER

REVERSE

BEAR image
H & G
(Heller & Garrett)

Richard Siri Collection

CALIFORNIA SELTZER WATER

FACE

CALIFORNIA
SELTZER WATER

REVERSE

Walking Bear
B & G
("B" Byam?)
("G" William T. Garrett)

1875 Quart from Cloverdale
States B & G instead of H & G

Courtesy of American Bottle Auctions
Jeff Wichmann

CALISTOGA HOT SPRINGS

Again a Native American area that was invaded by Anglo's in the 1840's. The area was abundant with oak trees that provided acorns and spiritual and medicinal healing grounds for the native band of Wappo Indians.

Samuel Brannan a co-leader of Mormon's with Brigham Young split off from the main Morman party in Utah and headed to San Francisco. He published the California Star newspaper and during the discovery of gold in 1849 he purchased large tracks of land in San Francisco selling lots and is thought to be California's first millionaire.

He purchased over 2,000 acres in the Napa area that had springs on the land and wanted to name it "Sarifornia" in reference to both the California springs and Saratoga Springs in New York. He opened his springs in 1862 which are now known as Indian Springs in downtown Calistoga.

Brannan built the Napa Valley Railroad Company providing customers a train to his destination from the ferry. Today the track is used by the Napa Wine Train.

In 1920 Giuseppe Musante who owned a soda fountain and candy store drilled a well for cold water but tapped into hot water instead and in 1924 started bottling and selling Calistoga Sparkling Mineral Water.

Elwood Sprenger purchased the bottling company in 1970 which became known as Calistoga Water Company.

SAMUEL BRANNAN

NECK "THE PERFECT MIXER" FACE NET CONTENTS 7 FL. OZ. CALISTOGA SPARKLING MINERAL WATER Gold Seals		REVERSE CHEMICAL ANALYSIS * QUALITATIVE BASES COMBINED LIME, MAGNESIA SODA, IRON, LITHIUM BY SPECTROSCOPE ACIDS COMBINED SULPHATES CHLORIDE SILICA CALISTOGA MINERAL WATER CO. CALISTOGA, CALIFORNIA

Calistoga Sparkling Mineral Water bottle available in quarts also.

CALISTOGA BOTTLING WORKS

FACE

CALISTOGA BOTTLING WKS.
(Monogram)
G. MUSANTE
CALISTOGA, CAL.

REVERSE

Blank

Giuseppe Musante operated a candy store in Calistoga at the Railroad Exchange and drilled for cold tap water and inadvertently struck a hot springs. In 1924 he began bottling Calistoga Mineral Water. He sold the business to Elwood Springer in 1927.

CALISTOGA SELTZER BOTTLES

CALISTOGA
MINERAL WATER
AND
BOTTLING WORKS
CALISTOGA,
CALIF.
CONTENTS MORE THAN 32 OZS.

CALISTOGA SELTZER BOTTLES

**CALISTOGA
MINERAL WATER
AND
BOTTLING WORKS
CALISTOGA,
CALIF.
NET CONTENTS 35 OZ.**

COLUMBIA

This bottle is considered from Walter's Spring's because like Golden West there were no such springs. It is believed that this brand was bottled and sold by George L. Abel who was an agent for Walters Napa Soda Water from 1892 until 1894.vAbel's office was at 641 Mission Street in San Francisco.

COLUMBIA
SODA
WORKS
S. F.

FACE

COLUMBIA
SODA
WORKS
S. F.

REVERSE

BLANK

Courtesy of American Bottle Auction
Jeff Wichmann

DUNCAN SPRINGS

**Cabin at Duncan Springs today.
John Louder photo**

Duncan Springs is located 1½ miles southwest of Hopland. I don't believe that they bottled water. The resort opened in the 1880's and the above cabin is still standing.

EL TORO SODA SPRINGS
NOVATO

Quoting from Waring's "Springs of California", 1915, "Mildly sulphureted water issues at El Toro Spring on the eastern side of a basaltic hill 2 1/2 miles northwest of Novato. This water was formerly bottled and sold for table use, but for a number of years it has been used only for domestic purposes. The spring rises in a stone basin, and its yield, which is about 4 gallons a minute, is piped to a storage tank 100 yards away, near the house."

Information from Eric McGuire leads to Waring's 1915 book "Springs of California"

FETTERS HOT SPRINGS

Rancho Agua Caliente, a Mexican land grant is on the east side of Sonoma Creek approximately 2½ miles from the town of Sonoma. Thaddeus Leavenworth purchased 320 acres of the current township of Agua Caliente in 1849. The local name of the springs in the 1840/50's was "Old Indian Medicine spring." The springs became known as Hotel Eleda Hot Springs selling to George & Emma Fetters in 1908

Even though they never bottled water at Fetters it was a favorite of mine when Juanita Musson owned a restaurant there; Juanita's. If you never met Juanita nor been to one of her many restaurants you missed one of Sonoma, Marin and Contra Costa's County's treasures.

Two postcards. Notice the growth and vegetation around Fetters.

GEYSERS SONOMA COUNTY

Native Americans discovered the Geysers and used the hot water and steam for healing and cooking of food. In 1847 John Fremont came across them while surveying for the United States Government.

The Geysers located approximately 12 miles southeast of Cloverdale were purchased by Archibald Godwin who built the Geyser Resort Hotel creating a tourist business. Because of the rough road and travel by stage coach his business declined. There were also other alternatives to people as other springs were being developed and much easier to travel too.

The main building was destroyed in 1938 by a landslide however the bar, restaurant and swimming pool remained open until 1957 then partially open until the fire in 1957.

FACE

CALIFORNIA
NATURAL
MINERAL WATER

REVERSE

Monogram

Not positive that this California Mineral Water bottle was bottled by Godwin but it is from the Geysers as noted 12 miles from Cloverdale.

BERNARD F. CONNOLLY
Bernard F. Connolly of Petaluma also bottled water at the Geysers from 1875 until 1888.

BERNARD F. CONNOLLY

Bernard F. Connolly of Petaluma also bottled water at the Geysers from 1875 until 1888.

FACE

GEYSER SODA

REVERSE

CONNOLLY & B-t

FACE

CONNOLLY & B t o.

S F

REVERSE

GEYSER SODA

FACE

NAPA
SODA
B. F. CONNOLLY

REVERSE

NATURAL
MINERAL WATER

COMMON GEYSER SODA

FACE

GEYSER
NATURAL BOILED
MINERAL WATER

REVERSE

Blank

GEYSER SELTZER BOTTLE

**GEYSER
NATURAL BOILED
MINERAL WATERS**

John Louder seltzer collection

GOLDEN WEST SODA WORKS

Jules Somps and Jean Meillete were partners from 1892 to 1895 and listed as proprietors of the Empire Soda Works in San Francisco located at 2301 Buena Vista Street. In 1895 the business was taken over by Jules and son Peter Somps.

From 1895 until 1897 GOLDEN WEST NAPA COUNTY NAT'L SPRINGS was bottled by Eugene Herve and Pierre Somps. Their distribution location was located at 622 Laguna Street in San Francisco.

Here is the problem with the embossing; there was not a GOLDEN WEST SPRINGS in Napa County. It is believed that the water was bottled at Walter's springs.

Herve and Somps apparently used this label, GOLDEN WEST SPRINGS until 1901 when Frank Meillette joined Pierre Somps. Somps was located at 624 Laguna and Meillete's location was at 820 Buchanan Street.

Meillette was bought out by Pierre Somps in 1903 and Frank Meillette relocated to 1619 O'Farrell Street from 1903 to 1906 apparently closed because of the 1906 earthquake and fire.

Pierre Somps and Frank Paillet were partners of the Golden West Soda Works from 1898 until 1901. Peter Somps took control of the business in 1901 forcing Frank Paillet to relocate.

Paillet retained Golden West Soda Works and Somps partnered with Ernest Herves. Paillet located his business to 820 Buchanan Street in 1901/02 and relocated to 1619 O'Farrell Street until the earthquake and fire of 1906.

GOLDEN WEST SODA WORKS

FACE

F. PAILLET
NATURAL
MINERAL
WATER
S. F.

REVERSE

NATURAL
MINERAL WATER
FROM THE
GOLDEN WEST SPRINGS
NAPA
COUNTY, CAL.

FACE

E. HERVE & P. SOMPS
PROPS.
622 LAGUNA ST.
S. F. CAL.

REVERSE

NATURAL
MINERAL WATER
FROM THE
GOLDEN WEST SPRINGS
NAPA
COUNTY, CAL.

GOLDEN WEST SODA WORKS

J. Somps & J. Meillete bottle is similar to the two bottles above; F. Paillet & E. Herve & P. Somps bottles on the prior page. However, the bottle not shown bottle is Alameda not San Francisco.

J. SOMPS & J. MEILLETE
AGENTS
COR. OAK AND
BUENA VISTA AVE.
ALAMEDA

NATURAL
MINERAL WATER
FROM THE
GOLDEN WEST SPRINGS
NAPA
COUNTY CAL.

FACE

GOLDEN WEST
SODA WORKS
SAN FRANCISCO
CAL.

REVERSE

BLANK

BOTTOM

HORSESHOE

GOLDEN WEST SODA WORKS
Crown Tops

FACE

GOLDEN WEST
SODA WORKS
SAN FRANCISCO
CAL.

REVERSE

BLANK

BOTTOM

HORSESHOE

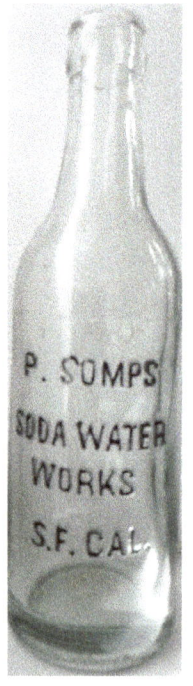

FACE

P. SOMPS
SODA WATER
WORKS
S. F. CAL.

REVERSE

BLANK

HAAS BROTHERS

Starting in 1873 until 1875 David Haas apparently bottled Napa Soda at Napa Springs until 1875 then became an agent for Jackson's Napa Soda until 1877.

FACE

NAPA
SODA

REVERSE

HAAS BROS.
NATURAL
MINERAL WATER

Richard Siri bottle

Also comes in colors
American Bottle Auction bottle
Jeff Wichmann

HARBIN SPRINGS

Sacramento Union
July 28, 1907

HARBIN SPRINGS

Of Lake County is positively what made California so famous as a health resort—by its great cures that doctors could not reach.

MAIN BUILDING, HARBIN SPRINGS

AREN'T you tired and worn out and need a rest? If so, why not go to the best resort in the world, where you can derive more benefit for less money than any other resort in the state? Elevation, 2000 feet, where the temperature of the hottest weather we have is only 86. Absolutely free from fleas and mosquitoes. All kinds of mineral baths, tub baths, mineral medicated mud baths, natural mineral steamroom and shower baths, swimming tank. Best water in the state for kidney, liver and stomach troubles. A positive cure for neuralgia, paralysis, rheumatism, gout, dropsy and skin diseases. Mountain trails. Best equipped gymnasium in the state. Fine fishing and hunting close to hotel. Fine vegetables, garden, dairy and livery stable, all connected with hotel. Round trip to Springs at S. P. office, $7. Send for booklet. J. A. HAYS, Proprietor. Take stage at Calistoga direct to springs only 19 miles over one of the most picturesque roads in the state.

HIGHLAND SPRINGS

LAKE COUNTY, CAL.
The Finest Resort for Pleasure Seekers and Invalids in California

These springs having changed hands, the undersigned take pleasure in informing their friends and traveling public that they are now prepared to accommodate all who wish to make trial of their virtue, or visit the springs for recreation and pleasure. Unlike most of the Mineral Springs these are recommended through the entire year, the water being considered quite as potent during Winter as the Summer months.

The accommodations, whether of hotel or cottage, having been entirely renovated, with new furniture and new beds throughout, are not to be excelled by any place of like character on the West Coast, while the bathing facilities are as perfect as could be desired, and the undersigned feel confident that they can guarantee perfect satisfaction to all who may favor them with a call.

There are a number of springs admirably adapted for drinking purposes, among which are;
>THE POOL OF DIANA,
>>THE MAGIC,
>>>THE DUTCH,
>>>>THE COOL SODA SPRING

Which has no equal in the United States. The Highland Mineral Springs have long been known in the surrounding country as a favorite resort for invalids affected with various chronic diseases, and many remarkable cures have been effected that medical skill has failed to alleviate. A careful test, chemical and physiological, proves them to be the very best Mineral Waters in America, having a greater variety and containing the very best combination of

Mineral Salts for the cure of nearly all classes of chronic diseases arising from impurities of the blood or derangement of the secretions, etc., such as Rheumatism, Gout, Neuralgias, Dyspepsia, Skin Diseases, Liver, Kidney and Nervous Affections, and especially debilitated females.

An analysis (qualitative) has been made, showing several of the Springs to contain Sulphate Magnesia, Carbonate Manganese, Muriatic Sodium, Potassium, Silica, and Calcium – most of them containing a little Sulphur, and highly charged with Carbonic Acid.

There are little more than fifty springs – some warm; suitable for bathing as the water flows from the Springs. Invalids can choose the water that best suits individual cases, or as their tastes may indicate.

The locality is a beautiful one, very romantic, with a background of mountains, at the foot of which the springs break out on the banks of a Limestone creek, which flows from a canyon above, in a clear, cold stream of sweet water, into a lovely valley, where the Hotel, Cottages, Bath-Houses and improvements are made. Around the grounds are lovely hills and valleys, with beautiful groves of many kinds of trees, making the scenery charming and picturesque.

The Highlands are seven miles from Lakeport and Clear Lake, and four from Kelseyville. Fine fishing and hunting in the neighborhood for sportsmen. Good roads and easy access. Only sixteen miles from Cloverdale, the terminus of the North Pacific Railroad, connected daily by J. P. Clark's line of coaches direct to the Springs. Parties leaving San Francisco at 7 A.M. will arrive at the Highlands at 5 P. M. same evening.

The climate is one of the most delightful on the coast, being neither cold in Winter not very hot in Summer. The elevation is about 1,500 feet above tide-water.

It is necessary for those who visit these Springs for the purpose of being cured of any chronic malady to come with the intention of giving them a thorough trial; also, to obtain the advice of their home on matters of diet, clothing, and exercise, as he may know the individual peculiarities of his patients better than anyone else.

The season proper for visiting these springs for their medical virtues lasts till late in the Fall, and may be continued all Winter with great advantage, and perhaps better for some characters of cases that would do better after the throng has dispersed, as there will be every comfort provided for invalids through the winter.

Transient visitors who desire to examine the springs will be courteously shown everything of interest. Buy your through tickets to the springs.

SMITH & CLOUGH, Proprietors.
P. O. address, "Highland Springs, via Cloverdale"

SAN FRANCISCO CALL
June 17, 1894

HIGHLAND SPRINGS, LAKE COUNTY.
Round trip tickets................$8.
Fine hunting, fishing and boating. Beautiful scenery. Post, express and telegraph. Rates reasonable. Open all year. Write for illustrated pamphlet. J. CRAIG, Manager.   ap15 tf SuWFr

SAN FRANCISCO CALL
September 17, 1911

Lake County Automobile Transportation Co.

Passengers carried by AUTOMOBILE and STAGES from PIETA to HIGHLAND SPRINGS, LAKEPORT, KELSEYVILLE, SODA BAY, BARTLETT SPRINGS and UPPER LAKE. Fine mountain road. Time for lunch at Pieta. Charges on automobile extra in addition to regular one-way stage fare to Highland Springs $1.50, Lakeport $2.00, Kelseyville $2.00 and Soda Bay $2.00. Tickets on sale at office Northwestern Pacific R. R. Co., Ferry bldg., and 874 Market street, Flood bldg., San Francisco.

SAN FRANCISCO CALL
August 20, 1912

Lake County Automobile Transportation Co.

Passengers carried by Automobile and Stages from Pieta to Highland Springs, Lakeport, Kelseyville and Upper Lake. Fine mountain scenery over this line. (Special all rail and auto round trip tickets, San Francisco to Bartlett Springs and return, only $18, including trip across beautiful Clear Lake). Extra auto charge in addition to stage from Pieta to Highland Springs $1.50, to Lakeport $1.50. Tickets on sale at Northwestern Pacific Railroad Company, Ferry building, and 874 Market street, San Francisco.

SAN FRANCISCO CALL
June 23, 1912

THE QUEEN OF LAKE COUNTY RESORTS.

HIGHLAND SPRINGS

Opened on June 15, 1912, with grandest opening ever held in the history of this famous summer resort. Special chicken dinner will be served in courses every Sunday evening from 6:30 to 8 o'clock at 50c plate. Music by Highland Springs orchestra during lunch and dinner hours. Special efforts are made catering to week end auto parties.

Grand 4th of July Celebration
Amusements During the Day—Fireworks at Night

RATES—Tents, $12 per week; Cottages, $14 and $16. Main Hotel, $14, $16, $17.50.

FARE—S. F. to Highland Springs:
  Train and Stage, $6 round trip
  Train and Auto, $11 round trip

Special transportation rates to guests, as follows:

One week stay at Highland Springs, round trip from S. F., including stage, $7, by auto $9.50.

Those desiring these rates inquire of PECK-JUDAH, 687 Market st., or W. H. MARSHALL, Proprietor Highland Springs, Lake county, Cal.

When communicating with this resort, please mention The San Francisco Call.

SAN FRANCISCO CALL
August 23, 1912

HIGHLAND SPRINGS AT FOOT OF THE MOUNTAINS

Highlands is located at the foot of the mountains, with broad fields and level ground extending away for miles. Clear lake is only six miles away.

Highland Springs, in Lake county, is situated only two hours staging from Pieta. The road is the finest mountain highway in the state, and is an ideal automobile route. Horse stages and auto stages make regular schedules between the railroad and Highlands during the season.

There are 30 mineral springs, all of them noted for their curative powers. Excellent hunting can be had in surrounding mountains. Magnificent roads and central location make Highland Springs convenient headquarters for automobile parties. All kinds of indoor and outdoor amusements, such as tennis, croquet, shuffleboard, bowling, billiards and large swimming tank and excellently appointed bathhouse, with porcelain tubs, are enjoyed.

HIGHLAND SPRINGS AS IT LOOKS TODAY
Buried under water

HIGHLAND MINERAL WATER

NATURAL MINERAL WATER

Bottle in circle
TRADE MARK

Rick Siri bottle
Highland Springs research by Eric McGuire

HOBERG'S RESORT

The resort was founded by Gustav and Mathilda Hoberg in 1885 and featured a main lodge, over 100 cottages with tennis courts, a baseball diamond, game room, restaurant, golf course, and swimming pool, horseback riding and turned into the largest privately-owned resort in the northern California. They featured big bands on weekends in the 1940's & early 50's like Artie Shaw, Bennie Goodman, Tommy Dorsey, Ray Anthony, etc.

Even though they never bottled water it is considered one of the most famous of the lake County Resorts. Through the years it was run by four generations of family and sold in 1970. Hoberg's Resort on Cobb Mountain was destroyed in the "Valley Fire" on September 12, 2015.

HOWARD SPRINGS

C. W. Howard discovered the springs which are located 2 miles southeast of Seigler Springs in 1877. On property are 42 hot and cold springs where Howard build a hotel, wIth full restaurant and saloon, additional cabins and campsites. The property was closed in 1969. Howard bottled Lithia Water, Bohemia and Eureka bottled water brands.

SAN FRANCISCO CALL
August 29, 1895

HOWARD SPRINGS, LAKE COUNTY, CAL.
HOT AND COLD MINERAL SPRINGS OF great healing power. Will cure constipation, aid digestion and purify the blood. Terms $8 per week. Water doctor on the premises. Write for circular and further information.

SAN FRANCISCO CALL
August 1, 1907

HOWARD SPRINGS
LAKE COUNTY, CAL.
Cures all cases of kidney and liver trouble. 42 mineral springs. Hot sulphur and iron plunge baths. Magnesia tub baths. Reference: Any guest for the last 20 years. Rates, $12 to $16 per week. Fare from San Francisco $9 round trip. Leave San Francisco 7:30 a. m. via S. P. Send for catalogue or address J. W. LAYMANCE, Owner and Mgr., Howard Springs, Lake Co., Cal.

SAN FRANCISCO CALL
August 17, 1907

SPRINGS INCORPORATED

OAKLAND, Aug 17. – The Howard Springs Company, which is organized to conduct the Howard Springs Resort in lake County, and which will have its principal place of business in Oakland, filed articles of incorporation today. The capital stock is $50,000 and the directors are J. W. Laymance, E. E. Laymance and J. J. Scrivner, all of Oakland.

HOWARD SPRINGS FOR SALE
SAN FRANCISCO CALL
July 26, 1908

FOE SALE OR EXCHANGE
SAN FRANCISCO OR OAKLAND PROPERTY
THE FAMOUS HOWARD SPRINGS IN LAKE COUNTY, CAL.
$50,000 HOWARD SPRINGS LAKE COUNTY, CALIFORNIA
"THE SWITZERLAND OF AMERICA"

BATHS
CLEANLINESS IS HOLINESS.
NO RESORT IS PERFECT WITHOUT GOOD BATHING.
NATURAL HOT SULFUR AND IRON PLUNGE BATH.
NATURAL HOT BORAX BATH - NATURAL HOT MAGNESIA TUB BATHS

HOWARD SPRINGS, is the ideal health and pleasure resort, is most picturesquely situated amidst pine forests of Lake County. Elevation is 2,300 feet. Absolutely free from fog and the harsh summer winds of the coast. CLIMATE PERFECT. Excellent trout fishing. Fine deer and quail hunting. Daily papers and current literature kept on file. Post office and telephone on premises. Daily stage twice a day. HOWARD SPRINGS the foremost watering place in the state.

FIRST, - HOWARD SPRINGS has 42 different mineral springs; every mineral known in water for medicinal purposes. The MAGNESIA SPRING for stomach trouble contains the largest percentage of magnesia shown by any spring in the world. The temperature, being 106 degrees Fahrenheit, gives it a delightful, warm, soothing taste - just the thing for the stomach. With this spring the owner guarantees to cure most any case of stomach trouble. Can produce hundreds of testimonials of cures by this water. Acknowledged by leading physicians, who have sent their patients there, that these Springs produce the best results of any water known to them.

SECOND – THE LITHIA SPRING contains more of Lithia to the gallon than any other spring in the state of California. So says that eminent chemists, Prof. W. T. Wentzel, United States chemist, appraisers building, San Francisco. As a cool delightful taste and can be drunk freely at all times

In addition to the two above principle Springs there are 40 others, consisting of iron, borax, alum, soda, arsenic, lime, sulfur and every other desire. All of the springs and baths are within three minutes' walk of the main hotel.

No other resort in the state can furnish such a combination of medicinal mineral drinking water and mineral baths as can be found at Howard Springs, Lake County, California. Round-trip tickets from San Francisco and Oakland, $9.00 by the way of Calistoga, including one of the finest stage drives in the state. Take cars for Calistoga from San Francisco at 7:30 a.m. arriving at Calistoga at 10:30 a.m. connecting with stage and arriving at the springs at 4 p.m.

REFERENCE- Any guest of the Springs for the past 20 years. Further particulars apply to or address J. W. LAYMANCE, Howard Springs, Lake County, Cal.

FIRE AUGUST 15, 1926 and NOVEMBER 10, 1929

A fire that started in the brush near Seigler Springs spared the Howard Springs but destroyed the bath house and power plant at Bonanza Springs. However, November 10, 1929 a fire started in the Howard Springs lodge and destroyed all buildings on the Howard Springs property except two cabins and two bath houses. The facility was rebuilt operating through the 1950's when it was part of a coalition with Hoberg's Resort. Republic Geothermal Incorporated held leases for geothermal exploration on 1,300 acres including the Howard Springs property.

HUMBOLDT

Humboldt Artesian Mineral Water was bottled by Joseph Monroe in Eureka from 1893 until 1897. The well was located approximately a mile south of Eureka near the edge of the bay. Originally the water was bottled as table water not mineral water.

Joseph P. Monroe was manager of the Eureka operation and his family also owned Alonzo Monroe & Company in Eureka in the late 1870s, Ferndale Bottling Works, and Eel River Valley Soda Works in Springville (Fortuna).

- A. Monroe & Company managed by Alonzo Monroe (Late 1870's – 1887)
- Monroe Bottling Works in Fortuna managed by Charles Monroe (1888 – 1899)
- Monroe Cider & Vinegar Co. Ferndale managed by Charles Monroe (1895 – 1905)
- Monroe Cider& Vinegar in Eureka managed by John Monroe (1902 – 1910)
- Monroe's Distilled Soda Water managed by Alonzo Monroe
- J. P. Monroe Eureka Humboldt County managed by Joseph P. Monroe
- Eureka and Humboldt Bay Soda in Eureka (1900 - 1910)
- H. (Huck and/or Holbert) & M. (Joseph P. Monroe) late 1880's.

Steven Jackson of San Francisco was their agent.

FACE

HUMBOLDT
ARTESIAN
MINERAL WATER

REVERSE

E
U
R
E
K
A

C
A
L

HUMBOLDT
ARTESIAN MINERAL WATER

FACE

HUMBOLDT
ARTESIAN
MINERAL WATER
EUREKA, CAL.

REVERSE

BLANK

KENWOOD WARM SPRINGS

Cottages at Kenwood Springs
Sonoma County Library Collection

LOS GULLICOS WARM SPRINGS

Bathing pool at Los Gullicos Warm Springs
Sonoma County Library Collection

LYTTON (LITTON) SPRINGS

Sonoma County Library Collection

Litton Springs Resort was built by Captain William H. Litton in 1860's and in 1875 building a resort including a hotel, picnic grounds, tennis courts and mineral springs. On property there are two soda springs and a seltzer and Sweetwater spring.

There had been a contract with Bernard F. Connolly to bottle water on the property. In the 1890's a contract to bottle water was with

In 1900 the "People's Mineral Hygiene Company" of San Francisco headed by William H. Bone as manager bottled water until 1902.

In 1904 Litton was purchased by General William Booth who established an orphanage for the Salvation Army. The structure burnt down in 1919 and was restored in the 1950's and became a rehabilitation center in 1959.

Daily Star
May 18, 1875

Notice heading
P. N. EMERSON
WM. H. LITTON

FACE			REVERSE
CONNOLLY & Bro.			CONNOLLY & Bro.

Note that this is the same bottle used at the Geysers.

LITTON MINERAL WATER BOTTLE
Frank & Laurel Ritz Collection

FACE			REVERSE
LITTON'S MINERAL WATER			H E A L D S B U R G

LYTTON BOTTLES

(At times spelled LITTON or LYTTON)

FACE

GEYSER
SODA
SPRINGS

REVERSE

NATURAL
MINERAL WATER

John Louder Collection

FACE

LYTTON
GEYSER
SODA
WATER

REVERSE

NATURAL
MINERAL WATER

LYTTON BOTTLES
(At times spelled LITTON or LYTTON)

FACE		REVERSE
GEYSER SODA		NATURAL MINERAL WATER FROM LITTON SPRINGS SONOMA CO. CALA.

FACE

LYTTON SPRINGS
(Pelican)
SWEET DRINK
P. M. H. Co.
SAN FRANCISCO
C. H. R.

REVERSE

BLANK

LYTTON SPRINGS SELTZER

**L. B.
LYTTON
SPRINGS
WATER CO.
SAN FRANCISCO**

MARK WEST SPRINGS

Mark West Springs Lodge
Sonoma County Library Collection

Stage arriving at Mark West Springs
Sonoma County Library Collection

NAPA SODA

Soda Springs, Napa, Cal.

San Franciscan Phil Caduc had various business ventures; he was an agent for the Philadelphia Brewery of San Francisco, Pacific Congress Seltzer and soda water as well as Napa Soda. The Napa Soda bottles were embossed with his name on the bottle.

He was an agent for Napa Soda from 1873 until 1881 and then Louis LeLoy became the agent for Napa Soda.

According to Peck & Audie Markota after 1881 Phil Caduc had numerous businesses; Cobble Stone Company, Steam Soda Works, Paving Company, Benicia Cement Company, Patent Brick Company, and a Carbonized Pavement Company.

SITKA ICE AND NAPA SODA WATER.—Customers supplied from the wagons on leaving their orders at the office, No. 43 Third street, bet J and K. PHIL. CADUC, Agent for the American-Russian Ice Co. and Napa Soda Spring Water. Consumers of Napa Soda will please take notice that the bottles containing the genuine article are invariably painted white on the bottom. FILTERS FOR SALE. au2-1m2p

NAPA SODA

NAPA SODA
PHIL CADUC

FACE

NAPA
SODA
PHIL CADUC

REVERSE

NATURAL
MINERAL WATER

FACE

NAPA
SODA
PHIL CADUC

REVERSE

NATURAL
MINERAL WATER

NAPA SODA

Samuel Phillips owned the Phillips Napa County Soda Water Company 1898 until 1910. He had leased and been manager of Walter's Napa County Soda Water Company prior to 1898.

In 1902 he partnered with Isaac Spiro and formed the Popular Soda Water Company of San Francisco. Phillips stepped away in 1901 and in 1907 merged with Majestic Bottling Works of San Francisco joining Edward H. and John Goetze.

FACE

PHILLIPS
NAPA
CO.
SODA

REVERSE

PHILLIPS
SODA SPRINGS
NATURAL
MINERAL WATER

FACE

PHILLIP'S
NAPA
MINERAL
WATER

REVERSE

PHILLIPS
NAPA
MINERAL
WATER

NAPA SODA
Louis LeLoy

Louis LeLoy replaced Phillip Caduc in the Sacramento market as agent for Napa Soda from 1881 to 1884. He had been a barber in Sacramento until 1880 then opened a liquor and cigar store in 1881 on "J" street. He passed away in 1888 and his wife, Lulu, managed liquor and cigar business until 1898.

Sacramento Daily Union
February 26, 1866

LOUIS LELOY,
French Barber, 121 J street, bet. 4th and 5th. Hair-cutting, Champooing and Shaving, 25 cents each. Perfumeries and Toilet articles of all kinds. fe1-1m

Sacramento Daily Union
December 20, 1866

LOUIS LE LOY,
FASHIONABLE HAIR DRESSER, HAIR DRESSING AND SHAVING SALOON, No. 56 J street, between 2d and 3d. TO THE LADIES and HAIR DRESSERS!—Human Hair, Curls, Braids, Waterfalls, Wigs of every size, and Nets of every description; Real and Imitation Hair Goods, wholesale and retail; Perfumery, Porte Monnaies, Cutlery; Brushes, hair, nail and tooth; Cravats, etc. All Orders from the country promptly attended to. d2-1m4p

Sacramento Daily Union
January 5, 1881

GROCERIES, LIQUORS, ETC

LOUIS LELOY,
IMPORTER AND DEALER IN
Foreign and Native Wines and Liquors,
TOBACCO AND CIGARS.
☞ SOLE AGENT FOR NAPA SODA. ☜
No. 222 J street, bet. Second and Third, Sacramento.
fe10-4p1m

LOUIS LELOY BOTTLE

FACE

NAPA
SODA
LOUIS LELOY

REVERSE

NATURAL
MINERAL WATER

Sacramento Daily Union
April 19, 1888

The will of the late Louis Leloy was filed in the Superior Court yesterday and Clotide Leloy, wife of the deceased, through her attorney, Robert T. Devlin, filed a petition for its probate. The deceased bequeathes to the petitioner all of his property, both real and personal, amounting to something over $21,000, and makes her the executrix of the estate. Eight children are named as heirs-at-law and left to the care of the wife.

NAPA SODA

In the 1870's Napa Soda Springs must have been owned by Dr. J. Henry Wood who built a hotel out of valley stone. There are 27 springs on the property with six being used for commercial purposes. If a bottle has a "W" on the bottom, chances are that the "W" represents Woods.

One would assume that being a doctor much of his clientele were invalids or persons with illnesses.

The bottling operation was from ended in 1873 when Col. John Jackson acquired the property and began bottling Jackson Napa Soda.

FACE			REVERSE
NAPA SODA			NATURAL MINERAL WATER

Sacramento Daily Union
May 25, 1872

NOTICE.

NOTICE IS HEREBY GIVEN BY the undersigned to the agents and patrons of **The Napa Soda Water,** That he is the Sole Lessee of the Napa Soda Springs, and that one Dr. J. Henry Wood has no control or authority whatever in the matter of the sale of Napa Soda Water.
H. BURDELL,
m24-6t4p   Office, 18½ Geary st., San Francisco.

This is definitely a soda bottled by Dr. J. Henry Wood between 1870 and 1872. Thomas W. Fenn of San Francisco was an agent for Wood's from 1870 – 1872. Bottles are cobalt blue. An advertisement in the San Francisco Call in late 1872 gave notice that H. Burdell was the sole lessee of Napa Soda Springs and Dr. J. Henry Wood was no longer in control.

FACE

NAPA
*
WOOD'S
*
SODA

REVERSE
(Slanted)
NATURAL
MINERAL
T. W. F. AGT.

American Bottle Auction Photo
Jeff Wichmann

FACE

WOOD'S
NAPA
SODA

REVERSE

NATURAL
MINERAL WATER

NAPA SODA WORKS

Ed Henry replaced Manual Silva as agent for Jackson's Napa Soda Water in the 1890's. Henry owned a saloon in Napa from 1901 until it closed because of Prohibition. There he sold beer, wine, distilled spirits and the Napa Soda. I'm sure the Napa Soda was used as a mixer for his private label whiskey.

He was also an agent for Shasta Mineral Water and distributed many flavored sodas; Sarsaparilla, Ginger Ale, Orange Soda, Lemon Soda, and Cream Soda.

FACE

JACKSON
NAPA
SODA
SPRINGS'

REVERSE

NATURAL
MINERAL WATER

ED HENRY

NAPA SODA SPRINGS

The Napa Soda Springs were first enjoyed by the Native Americans. When where the springs first discovered is when then first Native American stumbled upon them centuries ago. The springs were beneficial to health and considered a major factor in healing of the mind and body and a spiritual retreat. They also became a host and gathering place for all to enjoy.

And then…………….. The white man came along.

Records show that George Yount (Yountville) was among the first white men to come across the springs. Born in North Carolina he was a fur trapper who migrated into the Napa Valley and came across the springs while hunting bear.

Amos Buckman claimed the 27 springs in 1855 realizing the therapeutic waters the springs contained. In July 1856 San Francisco Attorney Eugene L. Sullivan opened a hotel on property and Willard Allen was appointed manager. Amos Buckman and Sullivan started legal claims to the property in 1860.

Also in 1860 while Buckman was in Benicia working on legal proceedings to the property Wood and his associates attacked Mrs. Buckman and staff beating them and destroying the bottling works. Captured and identified Wood and the others were sentenced $75 and sentenced to 35 days in jail.

April 1861 reported in the Napa Recorder a legal battle regarding the property between Buckman and Sullivan verse John H. Wood and George Whitney.

Later in 1862 Whitney and Wood again were arrested for throwing Buckman out of his house. Seven days later masked men came upon the property and set the bottling works on fire. Whitney and Wood placed a $1,000 reward for the identity of the arsonist but no one ever came forward.

COURT PROCEEDINGS

SONOMA DEMOCRAT
November 13, 1862
DIFFICULTY AT NAPA SODA SPRINGS

It appears litigation has been going on for in regard to the rights of property at NAPA SODA SPRINGS. The following communications in the San Francisco bulletin is one version of the affair, and also an account of recent outrages committed:

Editor bulletin: A diabolical act was committed by the lawless band of ruffians who came suddenly upon the property at the Napa Soda Springs just after dark on Saturday last, November 1st and took possession of the buildings and improvements placed in the legal possession of the owners Whitney and Wood, after a long litigation through all the courts in the state, obtained final judgment in their favor giving them a perfect title to the property and full possession obtained, under a writ of assistance executed on Friday last.

The party disposed one Amos Buckman, who caused a warrant of arrest to be issued, and Whitney and wood together with all their employees at the springs, were taken to Napa city at night, leaving the family of Mr. Whitney, consisting of his wife and four children, alone at the springs, unprotected from the bands of ruffians who were gathered about the Springs with Buckman, making threats against the life and property of Whitney and Wood.

Soon afterward the dwelling-house was taken possession by Buckman, and then commenced a fiendish outrage, by breaking into the bottling house, ransacking the premises, robbing the office of $100 in coin, breaking up the machinery, cutting pipes and destroying fixtures in the soda bottling establishment, and finally setting fire to the building, a portion of which was occupied as a dwelling.

All was consumed, together with a carriage-house containing a valuable set of wagons and a buggy. Property was destroyed to the value of several thousand dollars. The new store-house lately built by Whitney and Wood was in great danger of being burned by the great heat from the adjoining burning buildings, and would have been consumed but for the heroic conduct of Mrs. Whitney, who, with the assistance of her female servants, succeeded in preventing the woodwork in the stone dwelling from taking fire by application of wet blankets upon the exposed portions. Immediately after the torch was put to the bottling-house, the cowardly fiends ran to the mountains. J. H. Wood.

SONOMA DEMOCRAT
March 4, 1865
DISTRICT COURT
February Term – Saturday

A CASE INVOLVING THE NAPA SODA SPRINGS
Amos Buckman v Henry Wood -plaintiff in this action, claims prior possession of the premises, from 1855 to 1862, under a pre-emption claim known as the "Willard Allen pre-emption claim," which claim in 1856, was commonly known as the "Soda Springs" and being about 5 miles from Napa city, in a northerly direction. That on 5 June, 1862, defendant unlawfully entered and ousted plaintiff on the premises and now withhold possession from him.

Plaintiff claims that the value of the rent and profits are great, to-wit: $8,000 per year, and that the defendants have committed great waste, and damaged plaintiff in the sum of $1,000. Plaintiff asked judgment for the possession of said premises, and for the sum of $9000, the value of the rents and profits, and for the further sum of $1,000 and cost of the suit.

Defendants deny the possession of plaintiff on 5 June, or at any other time since February 8, 1860. They claim to own the premises by a deed from E. L. Sullivan to George O. Whitney in 1858.

Defendants also deny that on June 5, 1863, or at any other time, they unlawfully entered and ousted plaintiff. They deny the waste and that the rents and profits are the value of $8,000 per year. Defendants claim that on February 3, 1860 George Whitney and defendant Wood, as tenants in common, owners in partnership, absolute the premises, and the defendant Wood, as the lessee of Whiting, has been in possession of said premises: also, that in 1860, defendant in this action commenced suit against this plaintiff, and the issues were fully litigated, tried, and determine, and the Court Judge that the defendant in this action should recover possession of the premises, and it was determined by the Court, that George O. Whitney and defendant Wood were the owners of the premises.

The testimony in the case is very conflicting. Buckman claims to hold by pre-emption. From the testimony, that 1854, one Willard Allen went upon the premises where there were two or three soda Springs, from which the track took its name. In 1855, Backman and Eugene L. Sullivan made an arrangement with Allen, by which a hotel was built, soon after burned down, and also they improved the springs.

After the hotel burnt down, a settlement was had, by which Sullivan got the place. Upon this, as well as some other points, there is a conflict of testimony. The testimony of the surveyors, shows a conflict in the boundary lines; one survey reporting to include the springs, the other not.

A great amount of testimony was abducted, occupying the time of the Court for three days, commencing on Wednesday and being submitted to the jury late on Friday night. About 3 o'clock the jury came in with a verdict for plaintiff, and damages in the sum of $8,000. Woods retained the rights to Napa Soda Springs.

RETRIAL

SONOMA DEMOCRAT
OCTOBER 3, 1865
District Court J. B. Southard Judge
Amos Buckman vs J. H. Wood et al; on trial.

The jury after being out all night presented a verdict, this morning in favor of defendants. This action was brought to recover possession of the Napa Soda Springs, with about 15 acres of land, property worth about $100,000, now in possession of Dr. Wood.

This property is 5½ miles north of Napa City. The case was tried at the February Term of this Court, and a verdict rendered in favor of the plaintiff, which was set aside and ordered a new trial. The principle point of dispute is the boundary lines of the track, plaintiff alleging that the land of defendants does not embrace the springs and improvements, and the defendants allege it does.

Defendants claim under Willard Allen, who settled on the land in 1854, and by first of several conveyances from Buckman, Sullivan and Allen. Plaintiff claims those conveyances do not embrace the land described in his complaint. There was a good deal of conflicting testimony. The north-east corner of the land is a large clump of laurels. It appears there were two clumps of laurels, and it is very important to know which is meant.

This appears difficult to ascertain, as they have been destroyed by fire since the survey. Running from one of the clumps would embrace the springs, and from the other would not. This land has been in dispute a long time, and a great deal of money has been spent. Buckman was put out of possession in 861, and has remained out ever since; he now sues to be let in. The case has occupied three days in the trial, and a vast amount of testimony has been taken. It is ordered that a stay of proceedings be had for twenty days to prepare a statement on motion for a new trial.

JACKSON NAPA SODA

Having settled the court cases, Wood began bottling NAPA SODA from the springs and franchised out to both Phillip Caduc and J. J. Walters in 1862. Caduc continued bottling at the springs even after it was purchased by Col. John P. Jackson supplying the Sacramento Valley. Walters continued until he discovered his own springs in Pope Valley in 1872.

Col. John P. Jackson purchased the Napa Soda Springs April 1872 for $20,000 and invested heavily in the property. He renovated the property and advertised heavily in the San Francisco Bay Area touting the peaceful Napa property and the mineral waters health benefits. He improved the stage coach road so that it would also handle auto traffic.

The bottling plant was rejuvenated with the newest modern equipment available at the time. Mineral water was bottled and capped on site producing up to 4,000 bottles per day. He allotted permits to agents to represent Napa Soda Water and supply various California areas. The water was advertised to be drunk straight, plain lemonade or as a mixer for alcoholic beverages.

John P. Jackson died during an operation for Kidney Stones on September 26, 1900.

Permits to various agents by Col. John P. Jackson to bottle and sell
NAPA SODA with names embossed on bottle:

- B. F. Connolly of Petaluma — 1873 – 1885
- Fred Michaelis of Vallejo — 1873 – 1885
- M. A. Satterley & A. J. Page of Southern California — 1873 - 1885
- Manual Silva Napa City — 1878 - 1890
- Ed Henry of Napa City — 1901 – 1906

Permits to various agents by John P. Jackson to bottle and sell NAPA SODA
with initials embossed on bottom of bottle:

- Cutler & Pearson San Francisco (C & P on bottom of bottle) — 1882 – 1883
- William A. Brown & Co. San Francisco (B & Co. on bottom of bottle) — 1886 - 1887
- Bresson (A & B on back of bottle) — 1880's

Permits by John P. Jackson to various agents to sell NAPA SODA
without their identity on the standard bottle:

- Andrew Jackson San Francisco — 1873 – 1874
- Edward Jefferies San Francisco — 1876 – 1877
- John T. Ward San Francisco — 1878 – 1882
- Charles H. Jackson San Francisco — 1888 – 1889
- George H. T. Jackson San Francisco — 1892 - 1906

POSTCARDS OF NAPA SODA SPRINGS

FABULOUS 1906 JACKSON'S NAPA SODA CALENDAR

Calendar with permission and courtesy of Witherell Auctions, Sacramento, Ca.

NAPA SODA COMPANY STOCK CERTIFICATE
John P. Jackson, Jr.

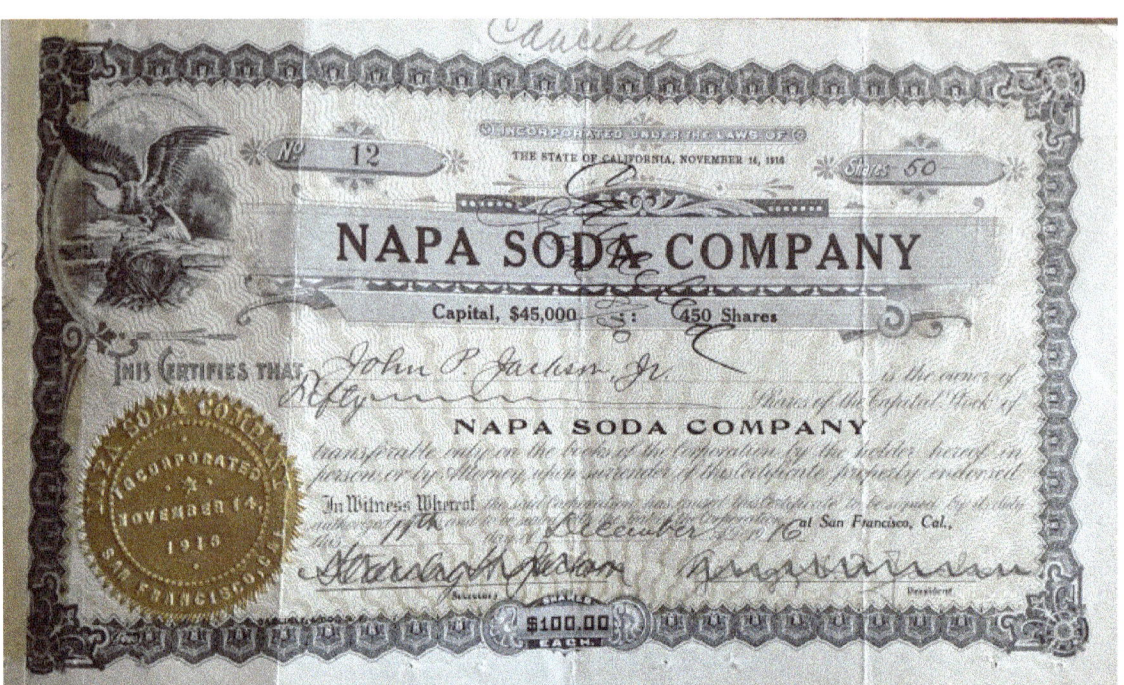

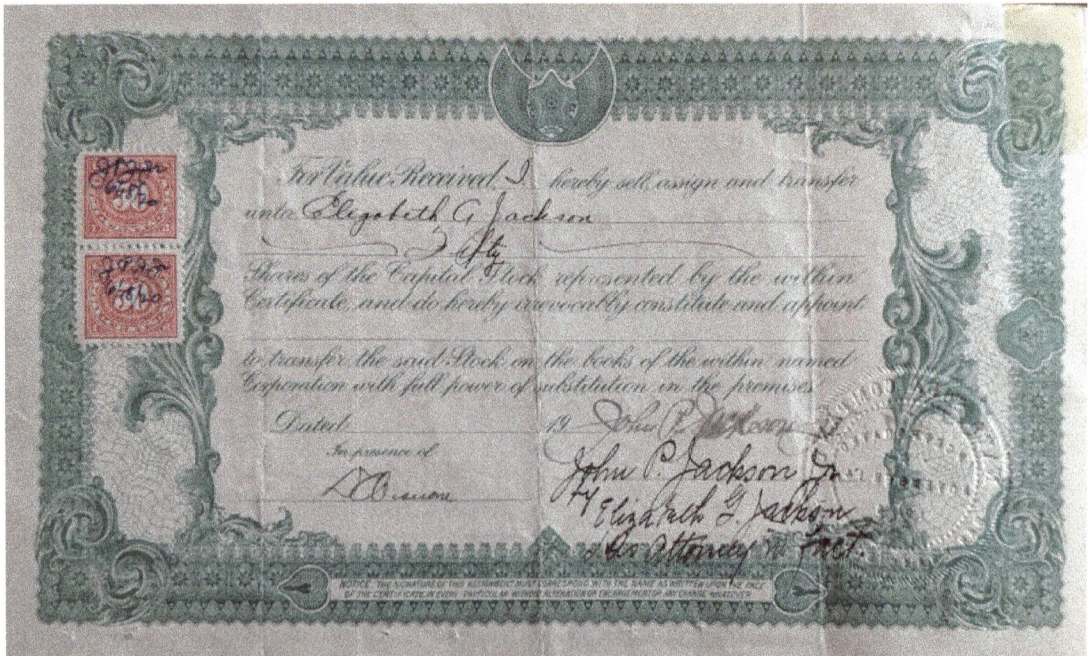

Newell Snyder Collection

JACKSON NAPA SODA SPRINGS MATCH SAFE

Match Safe Closed

Match Safe Open

Richard Siri Collection

JACKSON NAPA SODA PINT BOTTLES
Embossing same on both bottles

FACE

JACKSON'S
NAPA SODA
S. F.

Rolled top
Bottom 525

Crown top
Bottom 526

JACKSON NAPA SODA QUART BOTTLES
Embossing same on both bottles
Bottle on left has larger print than bottle on right

FACE

JACKSON'S
NAPA SODA
S. F.

Bottom 547

Bottom 548

Rick Siri collection

JACKSON NAPA SODA BOTTLES
AGENTS

FACE

JACKSON
NAPA
SODA
SPRING'S

REVERSE

NATURAL
MINERAL WATER

F. M.
VALLEJO

(Fred Michaelis)

Richard Siri collection

FACE

JACKSON
NAPA
SODA
SPRINGS'

REVERSE

NATURAL
MINERAL WATER

M. SILVA

JACKSON NAPA SODA BOTTLES
AGENTS

FACE			REVERSE
JACKSON NAPA SODA SPRINGS'			NATURAL MINERAL WATER ED HENRY

FACE			REVERSE
JACKSON NAPA SODA WATER			NATURAL MINERAL WATER

Bob Franconi Collection

JACKSON NAPA SODA BOTTLES
AGENTS

FACE

JACKSON
NAPA
SODA
SPRINGS'

REVERSE

NATURAL
MINERAL WATER

BOTTOM

C & P
(Cutler & Pearson)

JACKSON
NAPA
SODA
SPRINGS'

NATURAL
MINERAL WATER

BOTTOM

B & CO.
(Brown & Co)

JACKSON NAPA SODA BOTTLES

FACE

JACKSON
NAPA
SODA
SPRINGS'

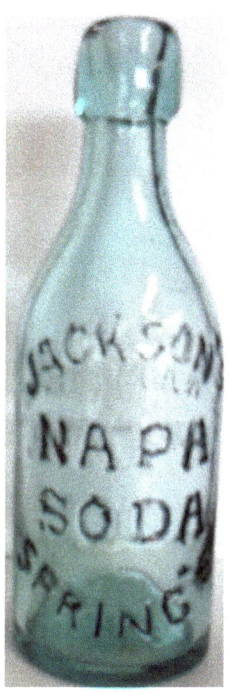

REVERSE

NATURAL
MINERAL WATER

FACE

JACKSON
NAPA
SODA
SPRINGS'

REVERSE

NATURAL
MINERAL WATER

THIS BOTTLE
IS NEVER SOLD

JACKSON NAPA SODA BOTTLES

FACE

JACKSON'S
NAPA
SODA

REVERSE

A NATURAL
MINERAL WATER
RECARBONATED
JACKSON'S (Angle)
THIS BOTTLE
IS NEVER SOLD

Bottle with closure
Richard Siri collection

FACE

JACKSON'S
NAPA
SODA

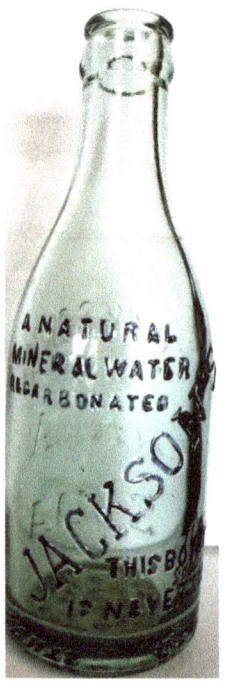

REVERSE

A NATURAL
MINERAL WATER
RECARBONATED
JACKSON'S (Angle)
THIS BOTTLE
IS NEVER SOLD

BOTTOM

CONTENTS
8 FLUID
OUNCES

JACKSON'S NAPA SODA
Paper label

John Louder collection

FACE: JACKSON NAPA SODA
SIDE: SAN FRANCISCO, CAL.

John Louder Ice Pick

PARKER HILL MINERAL WATER
SANTA ROSA

Parker Hill Water Production To Be Greatly Increased

Answering a steadily increasing demand, Miss Kate Parker has completed plans for marketing Parker Hill Mineral water on a larger commercial scale. Reduction in prices of the water in five gallon lots and the establishment of a downtown agency at the Nehi Bottling Works was announced as part of her campaign to increase sales.

The water, from the No. 1 well on the Parker Hill ranch, located four miles north of Santa Rosa on Parker Hill road, which intersects the Redwood highway in front of Lewis school, is a soft, self-carbonated sparkling water, and is syphoned direct from well to container.

City Health Officer E. J. Helgren has made numerous tests of the water to determine its properties, and the analyses have always shown desirable results.

Capacity of the bottling works at the well will be doubled to take care of the unexpected increase in sales, Mrs. Parker said.

June 30, 1935 Press Democrat notice

PARKER HILL MINERAL WATER
SANTA ROSA

DON'T SUFFER with liver, stomach and kidney troubles which cause many chronic ailments. Drink **Parker Hill Mineral Water** which contains certain minerals required to make the human system normal. LOOKS GOOD, TASTES GOOD AND IS GOOD. Rt. 5, Box 119. Kate E. Parker, proprietor. 4L20

April 1936 Press Democrat advertisement

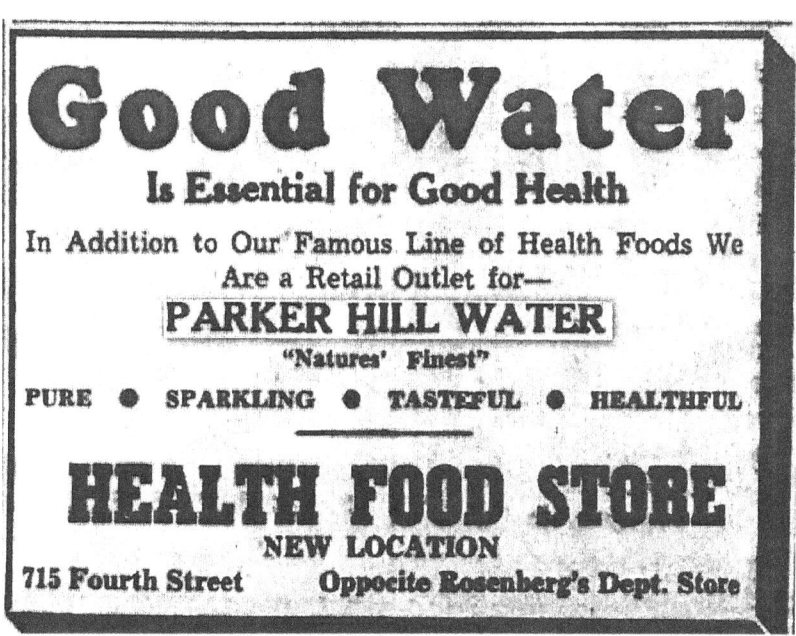

August 1944 Press Democrat advertisement

PINE MOUNTAIN MINERAL WATER
CLOVERDALE

TELEPHONE KEARNY 1442

Pine Mountain Mineral Water

BOTTLED AT THE SPRINGS BY THE

PINE MOUNTAIN MINERAL SPRINGS CO.

....Cloverdale, California....

OFFICE AND STOREROOMS:
715 BATTERY STREET — San Francisco

Business card Richard Siri collection

Pine Mountain Paper label

PINE MOUNTAIN

John Louder collection

POPE VALLEY

Located in the Napa Valley there is not much information regarding except this bottle is extremely rare.

Peter (Pierre) Guillaumes originally from the Spanish Pyrenees purchased land containing a spring in 1900 in Yountville 21 miles northeast of Rutherford. His spring was approximately one mile from Samuels Soda Springs.

Guillaumes had run the Swiss Hotel and a German Bakery in St. Helena prior to moving to Yountville. He purchased the Pope Mineral Springs and ran a hotel in Yountville which is still standing today. The hotel contained the Eagle saloon and he also was proprietor of the Rock Villa saloon also in Yountville.

Guillaumes began bottling in July 1913 in Pope Valley but hauled water in barrels to Yountville and bottled and carbonated the water there.

In 1907 a French relative John B. Lande from the French Pyrenees purchased the hotel which was along the side of railroad tracks and opened a butcher shop and steam laundry including a private residence. In 1936 the building was sold and became a private residence.

The Chef Thomas Keller operates the 5-star French Laundry Restaurant in Peter Guillaume's original location.

THE FIVE STAR FRENCH LAUNDRY RESTAURANT YOUNTVILLE

FACE

P. GUILLAUMES
MINERAL WATER
POPE VALLEY
NAPA, CO.
CAL.

REVERSE

BLANK

Bottle dates from 1913 to 1915

PRESTON

Preston California is just across the bridge north of Cloverdale. Owned and operated by John Kolling starting about 1910.

JOHN KOLLING
PRESTON, CALIFORNIA

Mineral Water   **Mineral Water**   **Cream Soda**

Root Beer   **Strawberry**   **Cloudy Orange**   **Orange Soda**

PRESTON, CALIFORNIA

Cloudy Lemon Soda　　　　　　　　　　　　　　　　　　　　　　**Lemon Soda**

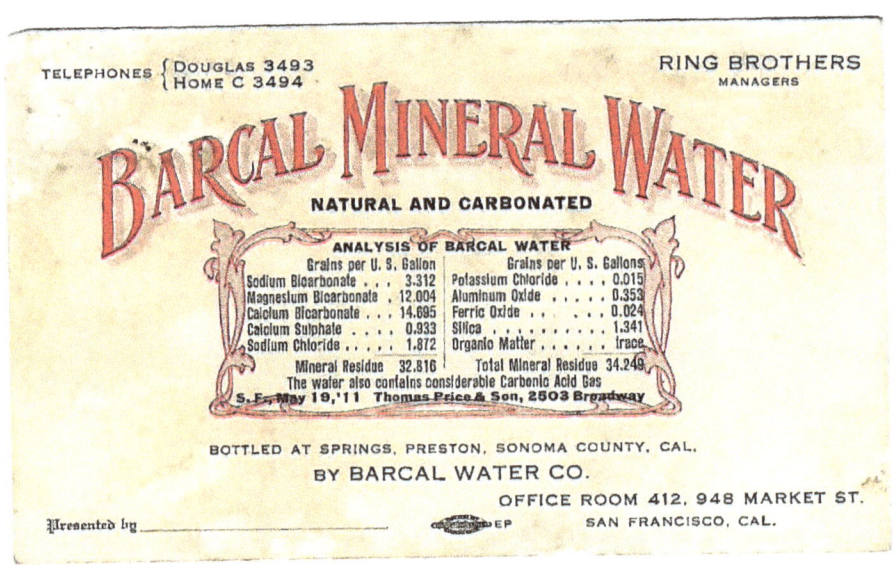

PRIEST SODA SPRINGS

Priest's Soda Springs and Farm

Joshua James Priest purchased his property from Hamilton J. Rayle in 1869 and operated his bottling plant from 1883 until he died in 1897. His son D. C. Priest then continued the bottling until 1899 selling the rights to Samuel Phillips. Phillips bottled the mineral water under his own name.

PRIEST SODA SPRINGS

FACE

PRIEST'S
NATURAL

REVERSE

NATURAL
BOTTLED
AT THE
SPRINGS
MINERAL WATER

FACE

PRIEST'S
NATURAL
SODA

REVERSE

NATURAL
BOTTLED
AT THE
SPRINGS
MINERAL WATER

PRIEST SODA SPRINGS

FACE

PRIEST
NAPA
VALLEY
SODA

REVERSE

NATURAL
FACE
MINERAL WATER

John Louder Bottle

FACE

PRIEST
NAPA

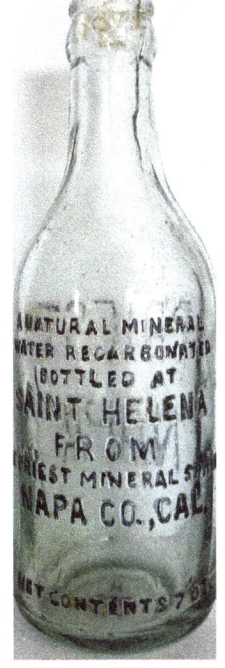

REVERSE

A NATURAL MINERAL
WATER RECARBONATED
BOTTLED AT
SAINT HELENA
FROM
PRIEST MINERAL SPRINGS
NAPA CO. CAL.

BOTTOM
366
H

PRIEST CROWN TOP

FACE

**PRIEST
NATURAL
SODA**

REVERSE

NATURAL

(FACE)

MINERAL WATER

SAMUEL MINERAL SPRINGS

Located on the northeast corner of Lake Berryessa is Samuel Springs operated by E. C. Samuels who claimed the property from the government in 1871. He started a bottling plant operated by water in 1886.

He built a hotel that could accommodate 125 persons and featured bar, dining, billiard and club room. The hotel featured a long distance telephone service, local newspaper and a mail service. Also on property were cottages, tents and cabins.

G. R. Morris purchased the property in 1891 continuing the operating including the bottling plant. On the *SAMUEL SODA Trade ^ Mark SPRINGS* bottles inside the "pyramid" were various initials. It is believed that these initials were related to each agent that sold the product.

"E. S." was for E. Samuels's and "E. S." on bottom of bottle
"A" was for W. F. Alexander in 1886 as trademark
"G" was for George H. Gregory in 1886 sole agent for San Joaquin County
"M" in triangle on face is for J. R. Morris who purchased property in 1897
    Eventually the company relocated to St. Helena

SAMUEL SODA SPRINGS
Registered Trademark
November 13, 1897

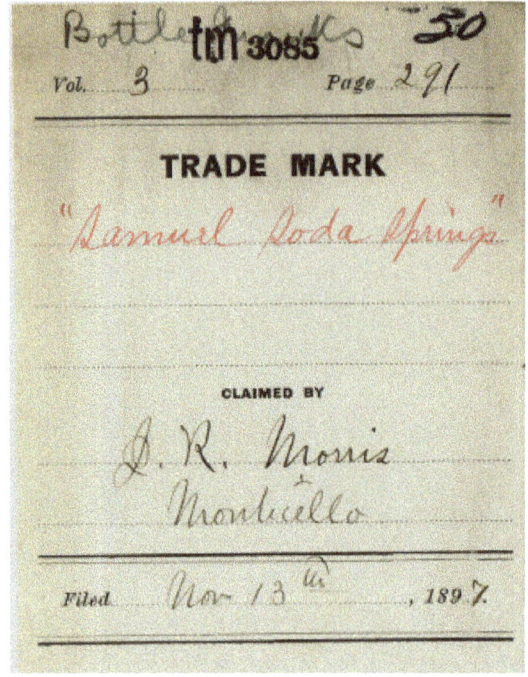

J. R. Morris - Monticello

SAMUEL SODA SPRINGS

1. The undersigned, J. R. MORRIS, is the owner and propri-
2. etor of the (SAMUEL SODA SPRINGS,) and as such proprietor is
3. engaged at Monticello, Napa County, California, in manufac-
4. turing, bottling, and selling soda waters, mineral and aerated
5. waters, cider, and other beverages, in bottles, siphons or
6. kegs, with his marks or devices branded, stamped, engraved,
7. etched, and blown, impressed or otherwise produced upon, such
8. bottles, siphons or kegs, and,
9. Under that certain Act of the Legislature, entitled, "An
10. Act to protect the owners of bottles, boxes, siphons, and
11. kegs used in the sale of soda waters, porter, ale, cider, [mineral or aerated waters,]
12. ginger ale, milk, cream, small beer, lager beer, weiss beer,
13. beer, still beer or other beverages", approved March 31st,
14. 1891, the said J. R. MORRIS makes the following description,
15. and gives the following notice:
16. NOTICE is hereby given by the said J. R. MORRIS,
17. proprietor of the said SAMUEL SODA SPRINGS, under and pursu-
18. ant to said Act, that, in his said business, he uses the
19. following names, other marks and devices, blown, impressed, or
20. otherwise produced upon the bottles in which his said bever-
21. ages are bottled or sold, to wit:
22. Upon the surface of the bottle is blown or impressed on
23. the side thereof in a curved line the word "SAMUEL", and be-
24. neath the same in a straight line is the word "SODA", and be-
25. neath the latter is the design of a triangle with the letter
26. "M" in the center, and to the left of the triangle in a
27. straight line is the word "TRADE" and to the right in a
28. straight line is the word "MARK", and beneath the triangle

State of California,
County of Napa.

I, N. W. COLLINS, County Clerk in and for the County of Napa, State of California, and ex-officio clerk of the Superior Court in and for said County, do hereby certify the foregoing to be a full true and correct copy of _Description and Notice of Names_ _Marks and Devices on Bottles, Siphons and Kegs by J. R. Morris, (Samuel Soda Springs)_ as the same appears of record in my office, with the original of which said copy has been compared by me and is a correct transcript therefrom.

IN WITNESS WHEREOF, I have hereunto set my hand and affixed the Seal of the said Court, at my office in the City of Napa, this 11th day of November A. D. 1897

N. W. Collins County Clerk,
and ex-officio Clerk of Superior Court

By _____ Deputy Clerk

SAMUEL SODA SPRINGS

FACE

SAMUEL
SODA
TRADE ^M^ MARK
SPRING'S

REVERSE

NATURAL
MINERAL WATER

FACE

SAMUEL
SODA
TRADE ^M^ MARK
SPRING'S

REVERSE

NATURAL
MINERAL WATER

BOTTOM

S & O
(Samuel's & ????)

"M" in triangle on face is for J. R. Morris who purchased the property in 1897

SAMUEL SODA SPRINGS

FACE

SAMUEL
SODA
TRADE ^M^ MARK
SPRING'S

REVERSE

NATURAL
MINERAL WATER

BOTTOM
E - S

FACE

SAMUEL'S
SODA
TRADE ^M^ MARK
SPRING'S

REVERSE

NATURAL
MINERAL WATER

BOTTOM
E – S

"E. S." was for E. Samuels's and "E. S." on bottom of bottle

SAMUEL SODA SPRINGS

FACE

SAMUEL'S
SODA
TRADE A MARK
SPRING'S

REVERSE

NATURAL
MINERAL WATER

Large "A" in box represents W. F. Alexander agent
John Louder Bottle

FACE

SAMUEL'S
NAPA
TRADE A MARK
SODA
SPRING'S

REVERSE

NATURAL
MINERAL WATER
A & B

Small "A" in box represents W. F. Alexander agent

SAMUEL SODA SPRINGS

FACE

SAMUEL'S
NAPA
SPRING'S

REVERSE

NATURAL
MINERAL WATER

FACE

SAMUEL
SODA
BOTTLING
WORKS
ST. HELENA

REVERSE

BLANK

SAMUEL SODA BOTTLING WORKS ST. HELENA

Same embossing on both quart bottles
Left bottle mineral top & right bottle crown top

FACE

SAMUEL SODA
NATURAL
MINERAL WATER

BOTTOM
E & S

Rick Siri collection

SAMUEL SPRINGS MINERAL SELTZER BOTTLES
Seltzer bottles from John Louder Collection

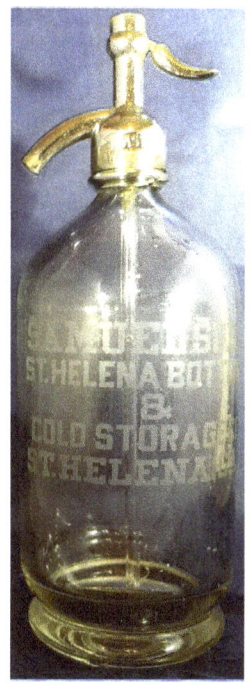

John Louder Seltzer Bottles

SEIGLER SPRINGS

Napa Register Photo

20 Miles north of Healdsburg situated in 5 miles south of Clear Lake in Lake County are Seigler Springs. The area was discovered in the 1870's by Thomas Seigler who built a resort including a hotel providing food, beverage and Seigler Mineral water.

A post office opened in 1904 closed quickly in 1907 but reopened in 1909 closing a second time in 1911. Population must have fluctuated a great deal as the post office reopened a third time from 1915 to 1969.

In the 1930's management was Captain Gudmund and Frank Hoberg. Frank Hoberg left in the late 30's and went to work at his family's resort; Hoberg's.

SEIGLER SPRINGS

THE IDEAL MINERAL MIXER
Bottled by Hoberg's
Seigler Spring's, Lake County, Cal.

SHADOW SPRINGS
MINERAL WATER
E. MARTINONI
SHADOW SPRINGS

PAPER LABEL

SHADOW SPRINGS
(Scene)
MINERAL WATER
NAPA COUNTY
E. MARTINONI

SKAGGS SPRINGS

Though they never bottled water these great photos taken in 1908 express the look of a majority of the springs at that time.

Photos courtesy of Sonoma County Library

SKAGGS SPRINGS

Skaggs Springs Stag leaving Geyserville Hotel
Sonoma County Library Collection

Skaggs Springs Resort about 1905
Sonoma County Library Collection

TAMALPAIS

Tamalpais label courtesy Newall Snyder collection

FACE

MT. TAMALPIAS
NATURAL
MINERAL
WATER CO.
SAN RAFAEL CAL.

REVERSE

A MILD
MINERAL WATER
T TAMALPIAS M
R SODA A
A FREE FROM ALL R
D DELETERIOUS K
E INGREDIENTS

TOLENAS SODA SPRINGS

Located five miles north of Suisun in Solano County next to the onyx quarries on the Armijo Rancho. Reached by rail from Sacramento or San Francisco to Suisun then a short ride by stage.

Tolenas water was bottled starting in 1885 until 1906. Some of the bottles have T. BROS. embossed on the bottom of the bottle.

Charles Eggers and Sidney S. Gould were agents from 1887 to 1903 in San Francisco. From 1903 to 1906 Tolenas Water Company distributed their own product in San Francisco until the Earthquake and Fire.

FACE

TOLENAS
SODA
SPRINGS

REVERSE

NATURAL
MINERAL WATER

John Louder has a Tolenas bottle acid etched with Astorg on back of the bottle. Astorg apparently purchased bottles from Tolenas or pirated them.

VICHY SPRINGS

FACE

VICHY SPRINGS
NAPA CO.
CAL.

REVERSE

NATURAL
MINERAL WATER

BOTTOM

S. F.

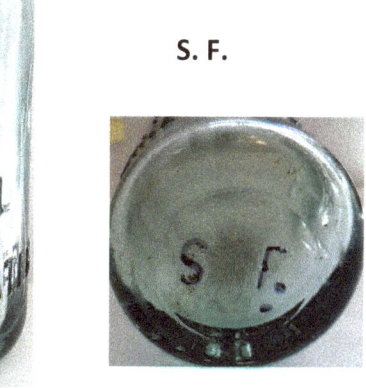

FACE
VICHY SPRING'S
NAPA CO.
CAL.

REVERSE
YOUNG'S
NATURAL
MINERAL WATER

John Louder Bottles

VICHY SPRINGS

Vichy Springs is located on Monticello Road a few miles northeast of Napa. The property originally was a part of the Rancho Yajome Mexican land grant south of the Silverado Country Club on Milliken Creek.

It is speculated that Young also bottled water at Vichy Springs from 1898 -1901 and as late as 1906 as his bottle is identical to his YOUNG'S NATURAL MINERAL WATER bottle except with YOUNG'S being added to the reverse.

FACE	REVERSE
VICHY SPRINGS NAPA CO. CAL.	NATURAL MINERAL WATER RECARBONATED

S F on bottom

NAPA VICHY SPRINGS

ACL FACE

NAPA VICHY
(Geyser)
A NATURAL ALKALINE MINERAL WATER

NECK STRIP

ALKALINITY
CERTIFIED
VICHY SPRINGS
NAPA, CALIF.

ACL FACE

NAPA VICHY
(Geyser)
A NATURAL
ALKALINE MINERAL
WATER
BOTTLED AT THE SPRINGS
1 FULL QUART

WALL'S SPRINGS
Mirabel Park

Wall's springs are located in a large ravine 14 miles northeast of Santa Rosa near the Russian River. There is a resort with a hotel and three cottages. There are five springs on the property with only one used for drinking water.

Sonoma County Library Collection

WALTER'S SPRINGS

Founded in 1871 by J. J. Walter who hired J. W. Smitte as supervisor. The main building housed a hotel with dining hall and there were also 6 cottages and a bathhouse on the grounds.

In 1879 patrons traveled by train to St. Helena then transferring to a stage and traveled over Howell Mountain to Walters Springs. The resort consisted of a hotel, dining hall with bar, and ...6 cottages.

1882 – 1894 Hutchins & Reynolds were agents for Walter's and where located on the southwest corner of O'Farrell and Mason Streets in San Francisco.

Not only was the water bottled at the springs by Walters, however, Somps, Phillips and Young obtained rights to bottle from the springs as well.

In 1885 the property was leased to Gustave Walter (a nephew?) and company then it was leased to Henry and Vina Conner in 1900.

Walter died March 15, 1901 of heart failure

In the 1950's it was owned and operated by Mabel Wise and in 1993 destroyed by fire.

WALTER'S

FACE

WALTER'S
NAPA
(Horseshoe)
COUNTY
SODA

REVERSE

MINERAL WATER
FROM
WALTER'S
SODA
SPRINGS

FACE

WALTER'S
NAPA
COUNTY
SODA
HUTCHINS
&
REYNOLDS

REVERSE

BLANK

WHITE SULPHUR SPRINGS
AKA
KAWANA SPRINGS

Among the first springs "discovered" in Sonoma County in 1862 which led to also having Sonoma County's first hotel. The land homesteaded by John Shackleford Taylor in 1853 established the area now known as Taylor Mountain. Taylor had been a pioneer who did well in the gold fields of California.

Taylor developed the property with 60 acres of grapes, both Mission and Zinfandel varieties, a small winery, and mined coal on the property as well. He raised trotting horses and developed a horse racing track. His hotel burnt to the ground in 1870 and was rebuilt immediately.

The Kawana mineral springs operated until the "Great Quake" of 1906 when Mother Nature abruptly closed the springs. Through the years the hotel was leased becoming a tavern and/or a road house. During Prohibition the "hotel" became a front for bootleggers and was raided by the federal Prohibition officers. With the 1969 earthquake a portion of the springs reopened closing again within a year.

Sonoma State Library collection

WHITE SULPHUR SPRINGS
VALLEJO
AKA
BLUE ROCK SPRING'S

White Sulphur Springs Postcard

The May 15, 1869 Vallejo Chronicle paper mentions that General Frisbee was the owner and made improvements on the hotel. There were also three cottages that had five rooms each. He had also built a two-story recreation room that included a dance floor, bar, billiard room, with plans for a bowling alley and shooting gallery.

WITTER SPRINGS

Construction began in 1905 and while partially completed the 1906 San Francisco Earthquake and Fire occurred and the contractor and construction crew left the uncompleted job and went to the city. They never returned to finish completing the building. They did bottle Witter water for a short period of time.

As with the main structure the grounds and the rest of the facility were never completed and there was never much business at Witter. The $250,000 building was sold in 1918 for $15,000 and torn down.

Rick Siri Paper Label Bottle

WITTER SPRINGS

NATURAL
MEDICINAL WATER
FROM
WITTER MEDICAL SPRINGS
CALIFORNIA

John Louder Bottle

WITTER SPRINGS WATER ANALYSIS

Some day this year you will probably want Witter Water

1951 CALENDAR 1951

ONE and the SAME
Indian History to 1863
"Tse-pa-ka-le-khi" — The White Oak Spring.

1863 to 1875
"The Deadshot Spring"
Valued by early white settlers

1875 to 1951
"The Witter Spring"
A natural alkaline water

WITTER WATER THOROUGHLY TESTED

"Witter Water" has been tested under the most exacting conditions by Inspecting, Testing and Chemical engineers and chemists for the purpose of determining the properties of "Witter Water" down to the most minute detail. "Witter Water" has been thoroughly tested in pathological laboratories to determine the effect of "Witter Water" upon the body. The value of "Witter Water" as indicated by scientific examination has been substantiated by clinical tests upon hundreds of patients by competent medical men.

But even before there were laboratories, or doctors, or even white men, the Indians, who knew the value of this wonderful water, came from many miles away seeking to rid their bodies of the evil omens which possessed them. Since 1875 people throughout the United States, Canada and the Hawaiian Islands have taken "Witter Water" to their satisfaction.

HOW MUCH SHOULD YOU BUY?

It is not reasonable to expect results from using "Witter Water" a day or a week. We, therefore, urge you to buy a supply of at least one dozen, or preferably three dozen bottles, of "Witter Water" which will last one person from three to four months by taking suggested dose. Years of experience have proven this period to be necessary for satisfactory results.

SMALL DOSE

Due to the high concentration of natural minerals in "Witter Water" the suggested dose, as determined by laboratory experiments, is only two ounces four times a day. No additional benefits can be derived by taking a greater amount. "Witter Water" thus becomes the "Thrifty Way".

PURE AS IT FLOWS FROM THE SPRING
Not a laxative — not a beverage
Get your supply of "Witter Water" today

MOTHER NATURE'S CREATION

By the magic of her touch, Mother Nature has created a small Spring whose waters are of such a nature that they must surely have been designed to benefit mankind. Nowhere in the United States or Europe is there another natural water containing the same quantity and diversity of minerals, as are found in this water now known as "Witter Water".

Scientific authorities say that even the most expert chemist cannot duplicate the exact manner in which these mineral ingredients have been combined by Nature. Geologists explain that "Witter Water" comes from unknown depths of the earth, where it has been subjected to tremendous pressure and intensive heat.

FUNCTIONS

One of the truly great functions of "Witter Water" is its capacity to neutralize the excess acidity of the stomach, thus relieving the pain and distress of excessive acidity. The buffer action of "Witter Water" reduces stomach acidity to normal, without impairing normal digestion.

Get your supply of "Witter Water" today

From

If your druggist cannot supply you, write to

WITTER MINERAL SPRINGS
Witter Springs
Lake County
California

WITTER WATER ANALYSIS
Analytical Report

Hypothetical Combinations	Parts per Million
*Ammonium Chloride—NH_4Cl	9.20
Lithium Chloride—$LiCl$	6.06
*Potassium Chloride—KCl	148.67
*Potassium Iodide—Ki	1.56
*Sodium Chloride—$NaCl$	848.84
*Sodium Sulphate—Na_2SO_4	6.89
*Sodium Bicarbonate—$NaHCO_3$	4057.90
*Sodium Metaborate—$NaPO_3$	3018.88
*Sodium Nitrate—$NaNO_3$	2.40
*Sodium Nitrite—$NaNO_2$	7.85
*Calcium Phosphate—$Ca_3(PO_4)_2$	2.46
*Calcium Bicarbonate—$Ca(HCO_3)_2$	620.10
*Barium Bicarbonate—$Ba(HCO_3)_2$	6.32
Strontium—$Sr(HCO_3)_2$	2.91
*Magnesia Bicarbonate—$MG(HCO_3)_2$	3060.19
*Ferrous Bicarbonate—$Fe(HCO_3)_2$	14.54
*Manganous Bicarbonate—$Mn(HCO_3)_2$	1.10
Alumina—Al_2O_3	1.00
*Silica—SiO_2	77.32
Total	11894.19

*Indicates elements of importance.

BACTERIAL EXAMINATION

Agar count: 37.6° C., 48 hours
- 0.01 c.c. No growth
- 0.10 c.c. "
- 0.50 c.c. "
- 1.00 c.c. "

B. Coli—48 hours., 10 c.c.—no gas.

Special: Media prepared with water under examination. (Reaction not adjusted inhibited growth of B Typhus.)

Summary: Water is sterile. Bacterial growth inhibited by contained salts.

Mother Nature's Creation

Witter Water

Rick Siri Advertisement

WITTER SPRINGS

Rick Siri Label

RECOMMENDED BOOKS

GRACE BROS. BREWERIES, HISTORY & MEMORABILIA
SANTA ROSA – LOS ANGELES – SACRAMENTO - FRESNO
John C. Burton
Aperitifs Publishing
Santa Rosa, Ca.
johncburton@msn.com

BOTTLE, TOKENS & HISTORY OF SONOMA COUNTY
John C. Burton
Aperitifs Publishing
Santa Rosa, Ca.
johncburton@msn.com

MARIN WHISKEY, BEER, & SODA BOTTLES
John C. Burton & John Louder
Aperitifs Publishing
Santa Rosa, Ca.
johncburton@msn.com

CALIFORNIA'S BEST
OLD WEST ART AND ANTIQUES
Brad & Brian Witherell
Schiffer Publishing Company
4880 Lower Valley Road
Atglen, PA. 19310

HERE'S TO BEERS
Byron & Vicky Martin
8400 Darby Avenue
Northridge, CA 91324

CALIFORNIA HUTCHINSON TYPE SODA BOTTLES
Peck & Audie Markota
Self-Publish
Out of Print

UNITED STATES BEER CAN GUIDE
BEER CAN COLLECTORS OF AMERICA
747 Merus Ct.
Fenton Mo. 63026

UNITED STATES BEER CANS
With OPENING INSTRUCTIONS
Kevin C. Lilek
Lilek Publishing
2828 Breckenridge Circle
Aurora, IL. 60504

THE NEVADA BOTTLE BOOK
Fred Holabird & Jack Haddock
14040 Perlite Drive
Reno, Nevada 89511

BOTTLES & EXTRAS
Federation of Historical Bottle Collectors
101 Crawford Street Studio 1A
Huston, TX 77002
emeyer@fohbc.org

AMERICAN BREWERIES
Donald Bull, Manfred Friedrich, Robert Gottschalk
Bull Works Printing Co.
20 Fairway Drive
Stamford, Ct. 06903
203-969-1925

SPRINGS OF CALIFORNIA
By Gerald A. Waring
1915
Book located at Santa Rosa Library Annex

AUCTIONS

AMERICAN BOTTLE AUCTIONS
(Jeff Wichmann)
915 28th Street
Sacramento, CA 95816
916-443-3210
www.americanbottle.com

WITHERELL AUCTIONS
Brian Witherell
300 – 20TH Street
Sacramento Ca. 95811
916-446-6490

SHOW CHAIR PERSONS

NORTHWESTERN BOTTLE COLLECTORS ASSOCIATION
Santa Rosa, Ca.
Lou & Leisa Lambert
707-823-8845
nbca@comcast.net

GOLDEN GATE CHAPTER BOTTLE COLLECTORS
East Bay Area
Gary & Darla Antone
925- 373-6578
PACKRAT49ER@NETSCAPE.NET

CHICO BOTTLE SHOW CHAIRMAN
Randy Taylor
P. O. Box 1065
Chico, Ca 95927
530-518-7369
RTJARGUY@aol.com

RENO BOTTLE CLUB
Marty Hall & Helene Walker
775-335-9467
775-345-0171
rosemuley@att.net

49er CALIFORNIA CHAPTER
BEER CAN COLLECTORS OF AMERICA
Corry Weidman-Sibell
antque1plus@gmail.com

AMERICAN BREWERIANA ASSOCIATION
P. O. Box 269
Manitowish Waters, WI 54545
715-604-2774

JUST FOR OPENERS
John Standley
P. O. Box 51008
Durham. NC 27717

SPRINGS OF CALIFORNIA
By Gerald A. Waring
1915
Book located at Santa Rosa Library Annex

A LISTING OF SPRINGS IN HUMBOLDT, LAKE, MARIN, MENDOCINO, NAPA, SOLANO & SONOMA COUNTIES

HUMBOLDT

Cook Spring	35 miles southeast of Eureka
Felts Springs	5½ miles northeast of Fortuna
Humboldt Artesian Mineral Well	1 mile south of Eureka
Mountain View Spring	28 miles southeast of Eureka
Sulphur Springs of Eureka	In Eureka

LAKE

Adams Springs	30 miles west of north Calistoga
Allen Springs	40 miles west of Williams
Alum Springs	49 miles north of Calistoga
Anderson Springs	22 miles west of north of Calistoga
Astorg Springs	30 miles west of north Calistoga
Baker Soda Springs	40 miles north of Calistoga
Bartlett Springs	44 miles west of Williams
Bonanza Springs	29 miles west of north Calistoga

Carbonated Springs

Southwest edge of Clear Lake	10 miles east of Kelseyville
In Scott Creek Canyon	7 miles southwest of Lakeport
Northeast side Clear Lake	7 miles northeast of Lakeport
Northwest edge of Clear Lake	8 miles north of Lakeport
Near Ranger Camp	45 miles north of Lakeport
On Bear Creek	43 miles east of north Lakeport
On Chalk Mountain	49 miles north of Calistoga
On Cole Creek	4½ miles south of Kelseyville
On Wiley Ranch	38 miles west of Williams

Carbonated Wells

At Kelseyville	Eastern part of Kelseyville
Near Upper Lake	½ mile south of Upper lake
South of Upper Lake	1 mile south of Upper lake
Carlsbad Springs	5 miles south of Kelseyville
Castle Hot Springs	25 miles west of north Calistoga
Copsey Springs (AKA Spiers & Complexion Springs)	28 miles west of Williams
Crabtree Springs (AKA Dennison & Hazel Springs)	38 miles east of north Lakeport
Dinsmore Soda Springs (AKA England Springs)	50 miles north of Calistoga

England Springs (AKA Elliott Springs)	8 miles southwest of Kelseyville
Epsom Spring	2½ miles south of west Lakeport
Gifford Springs	27 miles west of north Calistoga
Glen Alpine Springs	6 miles southwest of Lakeport
Gordon Hot Spring	28 miles west of north Calistoga
Grizzly Springs	31 miles southwest of Williams
Harbin Springs	20 miles west of north Calistoga
Hayvilla Sulphur Spring	5 miles northwest of Upper Lake
Hazel Springs	7 miles northeast of Upper Lake
Highland Springs	6 miles southwest of Kelseyville
Hoppins Springs (AKA Soda Bay Springs)	44 miles west of Williams
Hot Springs at Sulphur Bank	10 miles west of north Lower Lake
Hough Springs	36 miles west of Williams
Howard Springs	28 miles west of north Calistoga
Lee Soda Spring	6 miles southwest of Lakeport
Lyons Springs	6 miles north of Lakeport
Mills Hot Springs (AKA Castle Hot Springs)	25 miles west of north Calistoga
Morton Soda Spring	38 miles north of Lakeport
Newman Springs	45½ miles west of Williams
Paramore Spring (AKA Pearson & Saratoga Springs)	42 miles east of north Lakeport
Quigley Soda Springs	48 miles north of Calistoga
Richardson Springs (AKA Grizzly Springs)	31 miles southwest of Williams
Royal Spring	50 miles north of west Williams
Saratoga Springs (AKA Paramore & Pearson Springs)	42 miles east of north Lakeport
Seigler Springs	30 miles west of north Calistoga
Soap Creek Springs (AKA Newman Springs)	45½ miles west of Williams
Soda Bay Springs	5 miles northeast of Kelseyville
Spiers Springs	24 miles west of north Calistoga
Springs at base of Mt. Hannah	34 miles west of north Calistoga
Springs southwest of Chalk Mountain	48 miles north of Calistoga
Sulphur Springs near Blue Lakes	18 miles northeast of Ukiah
Sulphur Springs in Sulphur Valley	33 miles west of north Calistoga
Tunnel Spring (AKA Astorg Spring)	30 miles west of north Calistoga
Witter Medical Springs	20 miles north of east Ukiah

MARIN

El Toro Spring	2½ miles northwest Novato
Purity Spring	Near Sausalito
Rocky Point Spring	6 miles northwest of Point Bonita
Tamalpias Mineral Well	Downtown San Rafael

MENDOCINO

Artesian Springs	1 mile northwest of Hopland
Baker Mineral Springs	18 miles northeast of Willits
Carbonated Springs at	

Big Basin Carbonated Springs	15 miles west of Willits
Booneville	25 southwest of Cloverdale
Cantwell Soda Springs	18 miles northwest of Sherwood
Feliz Creek	3 miles west of Hopland
Garcia River	24 mile northwest of Cloverdale
Gobbis Soda Springs (Russian River)	1 mile southwest of Ukiah
Hazel Hill Carbonated Springs	5 miles northwest of Booneville
Humanity Springs (Russian River)	2½ miles north of Hopland
Long Valley Creek (Llewellyn)	7 miles north of Sherwood
Russian River (Hewett Ranch)	2½ miles north of Hopland
Shoemaker Dell Carbonated Springs	6 miles northwest of Ukiah
Snider ranch	10 miles northeast of Willits
Southwest Willits	10 miles southwest of Willits
Travelers Home Carbonated Springs	12 miles northwest of Willits
Wendling (Sterns Lumber)	25 miles west of Ukiah
West of Willits (Irvine & Muir Lumber Co.)	7 miles west of Willits
White Ranch	10 miles northeast of Willits
Duncan Springs	2 miles west of south Hopland
Jackson Valley Mineral Springs	18 miles northwest of Sherwood
Jackson Valley Mud Springs	19 miles northwest of Sherwood
Kinsner Soda Spring	11 miles northeast of Willits
McDowell Springs	5 miles southeast of Hopland
Muir Springs	4 miles northeast of Willits
Ornbauns Mineral Spring	20 miles northwest of Cloverdale
Orr's Hot Springs	16 miles northwest of Ukiah
Petersons Mineral Spring	12 miles northwest of Laytonville
Point Arena Hot Springs	15 mile southeast of Point Arena
Salmon Creek Mineral Springs	12 miles south of east Willits
Singleys Soda Spring	14 miles southwest of Ukiah

Sulphur Springs at

Near branch of Eel River	12 miles northwest of Laytonville
Near Cummings	30 miles north of Sherwood
Near Laytonville	½ mile north of Laytonville
Deep Creek	4 miles east of Willits
Vichy Springs	3 miles northeast of Ukiah

NAPA

Aetna Springs	17 miles north of St. Helena
Calistoga Hot Springs	½ mile east of Calistoga Depot
Congress Springs	3½ miles southwest of Napa
Crystal Springs	3 miles north of St. Helena
Guillaumes Springs	12 miles northeast of St. Helena
Jacksons Napa Soda Springs	7 miles north of Napa
Napa Rock Soda Springs (AKA Priest Soda Springs)	15 miles north of east St. Helena

NAPA CONTINUED

Napa Vichy Springs	3½ miles north of Napa
Phillips Soda Springs	15 miles north of east St. Helena
Priest Soda Springs (AKA Napa Rock Soda Springs)	15 miles north of east St. Helena
St. Helena White Sulphur Springs	2 miles southwest of St. Helena
Samuel Soda Springs	22 miles northeast of St. Helena
Springs at Veterans Home	2 miles southwest of Yountville
Walters Mineral Springs	16 miles north of east St. Helena
Zem Zem Spring	5 miles southeast of Knoxville

SOLANO

Tolenas Springs	6 miles north of Fairfield
Vallejo White Sulphur Spring	14 miles northeast of Vallejo

SONOMA

Agua Caliente Springs (AKA Agua Rica Springs)	3 miles northwest of Sonoma
Agua Rica Springs (AKA Agua Caliente Springs)	3 miles northwest of Sonoma
Alder Glen Springs	2.7 miles southeast of Hopland
Boyes Hot Springs	2 miles northwest of Sonoma
Eleda Hot Springs (AKA Fetters Hot Springs)	2¾ miles northwest of Sonoma
Fairmont Hot Springs (AKA Hoods Hot Springs)	15 miles west of north Cloverdale
Fetters Hot Springs (AKA Eleda Hot Springs)	2¾ miles northwest of Sonoma
Franz Valley Sulphur Springs	5 miles west of Calistoga
Geysers	18 miles south of east Cloverdale
Geyser Spa Springs (AKA Lytton Springs)	½ mile west of Lytton Station
Hoods Hot Springs (AKA Fairmont Hot Springs)	15 miles west of north Cloverdale
Kawana Sulphur Spring (AKA White Sulphur Springs)	2 miles southeast of Santa Rosa
Little Geysers	22 miles south of east Cloverdale
Little Sulphur Creek	6 miles northeast of Geyserville
Los Guilicos Warm Springs	3½ miles southwest of Glen Ellen
Lytton Springs	½ mile west of Lytton Station
Mark West Warm Springs	7 miles northeast of Fulton
McEwan Warm Springs	3 miles southwest of Kenwood
O'Donnell's Springs	north edge of Glen Ellen
Ohms Springs	2 miles northwest of Sonoma
Skaggs Hot Springs	9 miles south of west Geyserville
State Home Warm Springs in Eldridge	6 miles west of north Sonoma
Sulphur Creek	3 miles northeast of Cloverdale
Wall Springs	14 Miles northwest of Santa Rosa

www.ingramcontent.com/pod-product-compliance
Lightning Source LLC
Chambersburg PA
CBHW061149070526
44584CB00034B/4462